Teacher Develop
Over Time

Teacher Development Over Time: Practical Activities for Language Teachers addresses teacher learning over the span of the careers of both novice and experienced teachers in English Language Teaching (ELT). It is designed to a) help novice ELT teachers to see the ways in which their learning may open up careers and communities·over a professional life span; and b) support experienced ELT teachers in understanding where they are in their careers and how they may respond creatively to the challenges in that particular career phase. Part 1 synthesises views of major research on teaching as it is experienced over time by teachers and discusses the implications. Readers engage with these ideas via the activities in Part 2, which encourage them to reflect on their career paths and on possible themes for future work. Part 3 describes ways teachers can set the Part 2 activities within a busy professional life, and Part 4 helps teachers to engage in further explorations on their own or with others. By merging a strong line of research with very practical tools for understanding professional development, *Teacher Development Over Time* proves to be an indispensable resource for language teachers as well as teacher educators and mentors.

Tessa Woodward is Editor of *The Teacher Trainer* journal for Pilgrims, Canterbury, UK. She is a Past President and International Ambassador of the International Association of Teachers of English as a Foreign Language and founded the IATEFL Special Interest Group for Teacher Trainers (now the SIG T Ed/TT). She is also the founder of *The Fair List, UK* (www.thefairlist.org).

Kathleen Graves is Associate Professor of Education Practice at the University of Michigan, USA, where she works in teacher education and curriculum development. She is the series editor of the TESOL Language Curriculum Development series.

Donald Freeman is Professor of Education at the University of Michigan, USA. He directs the *Learning4Teaching* Project, a series of national research studies of ELT public-sector teachers' experiences in professional development conducted in Chile, Turkey, and Qatar.

Research and Resources in Language Teaching

Series Editors: Anne Burns, University of New South Wales, Australia, and Jill Hadfield, Unitec Institute of Technology, New Zealand.

Research and Resources in Language Teaching is a groundbreaking series that aims to integrate the latest research in language teaching and learning with innovative classroom practice. Books in the series offer accessible accounts of current research on a particular topic, linked to a wide range of practical and immediately usable classroom activities.

Digital Literacies
By Gavin Dudeney, Nicky Hockly, and Mark Pegrum

Motivating Learning
By Zoltán Dörnyei and Jill Hadfield

Active Listening
By Michael Rost and J. J. Wilson

Reflective Dialogue: Advising in Language Learning
By Satoko Kato and Jo Mynard

Teacher Development Over Time: Practical Activities for Language Teachers
By Tessa Woodward, Kathleen Graves, and Donald Freeman

Teacher Development Over Time

Practical Activities for Language Teachers

Tessa Woodward,
Kathleen Graves, and
Donald Freeman

Routledge
Taylor & Francis Group

NEW YORK AND LONDON

First published 2018
by Routledge
711 Third Avenue, New York, NY 10017

and by Routledge
2 Park Square, Milton Park, Abingdon, Oxon, OX14 4RN

Routledge is an imprint of the Taylor & Francis Group, an informa business

© 2018 Taylor & Francis

Library of Congress Cataloging-in-Publication Data
A catalog record for this book has been requested

ISBN: 978-1-138-20704-2 (hbk)
ISBN: 978-1-138-20705-9 (pbk)
ISBN: 978-1-315-46333-9 (ebk)

Typeset in Helvetica
by Apex CoVantage, LLC

To everyone who has shared ideas over the years and contributed to our professional development over time.

Contents

Lists of Illustrations   *xiii*

Series Editor Preface   *xiv*

1   From Research to Implications   **1**

    A.   Introduction   1

    Choosing Research That Is '*From* — Not *About* — Teachers'   2

    Three Researchers Who Have Studied the
       Trajectories of Teacher Development   3

    Organisation of Part 1   5

    B.   The Research: Key Ideas About Teacher
       Development Over Time   6

       1.   Dan Lortie, *Schoolteacher: A Sociological
            Study* (1975)   6

            1.1   About the Study: 'Where Teachers and
                  Students Meet'   7

            1.2   Key Ideas   8

       2.   Michael Huberman, *The Lives of
            Teachers* (1989)   17

            2.1   About the Study: "Several People . . .
                  Have Characterised This Research as
                  an 'Insane' Undertaking."   17

            2.2   Key Ideas   19

       3.   Amy B. M. Tsui, *Understanding Expertise
            in Teaching: Case Studies of
            ESL Teachers* (2003)   23

            3.1   About the Study: "What Exactly
                  Constitutes Expertise?"   24

            3.2   Key Ideas   26

       4.   The *Learning4Teaching* Project   35

            4.1   About the Studies   36

            4.2   Key Ideas   39

Contents

C. Implications of the Research: What We Can Learn
    About Teacher Development Over Time   45
    5.   Implications of Lortie's Study   46
         5.1 How Our Experiences as Students
              Can Help Us Understand the Ways We
              Teach (Apprenticeship of Observation)   46
         5.2 How the Work of Teaching Viewed
              From the Outside (One-Step
              Profession) Contrasts With How We
              Experience It (Egg-Crate Profession)   47
         5.3 How Teaching Is a Balancing Act
              Between Instructional Goals and
              Relational Work (Satisficing)   49
    6.   Implications of Huberman's Study   50
         6.1 The Amount of Self-Reflection and
              Professional Dialogue With Colleagues
              That Teachers Are Able to Do   50
         6.2 How the Themes Identified Could Be
              Used in Such Self-Reflection or
              Collegial Activity   51
         6.3 Whether All Teachers Follow the Same
              Career Stages and Trajectories as
              the Ones Described in the Study   51
         6.4 What Factors Could Constitute
              Pedagogical Competence   52
         6.5 What Attitude Towards Ourselves and
              Our Professional Colleagues Is
              Most Helpful   52
    7.   Implications of Tsui's Study   53
         7.1 How We Understand Our Own
              Histories as Teachers   53
         7.2 How We Relate to and Use Teaching
              Knowledge   54
         7.3 How We Relate to Our Teaching
              Contexts   54
         7.4 How We Negotiate the Relationship
              Between Theory and Practice   55

7.5 How We Sustain Our Professional
Learning   55
8. Implications of the *Learning4Teaching*
Project   56
8.1 How We Make Sense of Professional
Development Is a Personal Process   57
8.2 Professional Learning Involves Making
Sense of (and From) Learning
Opportunities   57
D. Looking Ahead   57

2. From Implications to Application   **59**
A. Introduction   59
Links Between the Research/Implications and
the Activities   59
Organisation of the Activities in Part 2   66
B. Where Have I Come From as a Teacher?   67
Activity 1: *How Did I Become an
English Teacher?*   68
Activity 2: *My Career Graph*   70
Activity 3: *What Are My Own Professional Life
Cycle Stages?*   71
Activity 4: *Material Changes*   72
Activity 5: *Methodological Changes*   74
Activity 6: *Ghosts Behind the Blackboard*   76
Activity 7: *Talking Shop*   77
Activity 8: *Yearly Retrospective*   79
Activity 9: *Critical Incidents*   80
Activity 10: *Language-Learning Autobiography* 81
Activity 11: *Transformative Times*   82
Activity 12: *Professional Development Survey* 85
C. Where Am I Now?   88
Activity 13: *How Do I Grow a Teaching Skill?* 90
Activity 14: *Checking Bad Habits!*   91
Activity 15: *Doing What Makes Sense*   94
Activity 16: *Exploring Dichotomies in Teaching
Knowledge*   95

Contents

Activity 17: *Teaching Knowledge as 'Either/Or' vs 'Both/And'*   96

Activity 18: *Facing a Difficult Stage in My Professional Life Cycle*   98

Activity 19: *How Can I Respond Creatively to a Difficult Stage of My Professional Life Cycle?*   100

Activity 20: *How Can I Check My Pedagogical Competence?*   102

Activity 21: *Letter to a Mentor*   104

Activity 22: *There Is Nothing So Practical as a Good Theory*   105

Activity 23: *Teaching Log*   106

Activity 24: *A Course Book Page We Love/Hate*   108

Activity 25: *They Keep Getting Younger!*   111

Activity 26: *How Do I See My Students?*   112

Activity 27: *Dialogue Journals*   113

Activity 28: *Building Case Studies*   117

Activity 29: *Freirean Problem Posing*   119

Activity 30: *Teaching Bump*   121

Activity 31: *From Tactics to Beliefs: The Four-Column Analysis*   123

Activity 32: *Constraints and Resources of My Teaching Context*   125

Activity 33: *Describing My Work*   128

Activity 34: *Half-Scripted Interviews*   130

Activity 35: *Writing an Op-Ed*   133

Activity 36: *Two Maps of Professional Learning*   136

D.   Where Am I Headed?   139

Activity 37: *Where Do I Want to Go Next?*   141

Activity 38: *A 'Good' Teacher Is . . .*   142

Activity 39: *How Do I Grow a Teacher Learning Technique?*   142

Activity 40: *What's in My Teaching Suitcase?*   144

Activity 41: *Who Is My 'Go To Person'?*   146

Activity 42: *Who I Could Become*   147

Contents

Contents

Activity 43: *Talking to My (Other) Self* — 148
Activity 44: *Mapping the Future* — 150
Activity 45: *From Known to New* — 152
Activity 46: *An Eddy in the River* — 153
Activity 47: *Graphic Organiser for Teacher Training and Development* — 154
Activity 48: *I Plan, You Teach. You Plan, I Teach.* — 156
Activity 49: *Finding Balance Then Staying Interested* — 158
Activity 50: *Breaking Rules* — 163
Activity 51: *Moving On: Collecting or Throwing Away?* — 165
Activity 52: *Moving On, Heading Out* — 166

3 From Application to Implementation — 169

A. If You Are a Teacher Who Prefers Working on Your Own — 169
B. If You Are a Teacher Who Prefers to Work Face to Face With a Couple of Colleagues — 175
C. If You Are a Teacher Interested in a CPD Programme in an Institution — 180
D. If You Are a Teacher Interested in Collaborating Across Local Institutions — 186
E. If You Are a Teacher Trainer About to Run a Short Professional Development Course — 188
F. If You Are Interested in Virtual Learning, in Personal Learning Networks (PLNs) — 194

4 From Implementation to Research — 195

A. Two Perspectives on Studying Teacher Development Over Time — 195
  1. A Research Perspective to Studying Teacher Development 'Over Time' — 195
  2. An Inquiry Perspective—Studying Your Own Development as a Teacher 'Over Time' — 199
B. Inquiring Collectively — 201

Contents

C.   Inquiring With Fellow Teachers   205
D.   Inquiring on Your Own   208
E.   Starting the Process   209

Appendix   *211*
References   *218*
Index   *223*

Illustrations

Figures

1.1 "Proposed core conceptual framework for studying the effects of professional development on teachers and students" (Desimone, 2009, p. 185)   38
2.1 Activity 32: Venn Diagram   127
2.2 "Conceptual framework for studying the effects of professional development on teachers and students" (Desimone, 2009, p. 185)   137
4.1 Two approaches to validity in studies 'over time'   197
4.2 Inquiring into teaching   208

Tables

1.1 Lortie's 'five-cell' research design   7
1.2 Huberman's model of themes in teachers' career cycle   19
1.3 Tsui's critical differences that characterise expert teachers   29
1.4 The design of the *Learning4Teaching* Project   36
1.5 National surveys in the *Learning4Teaching* Project   40
2.1 Lortie—Summary of implications and related activities   60
2.2 Huberman—Summary of implications and related activities   61
2.3 Tsui—Summary of implications and related activities   63
2.4 *Learning4Teaching* Project—Summary of implications and related activities   65
2.5 The premises underlying the design of the *Learning4Teaching* Project   137
4.1 Classroom research, Action research, Teacher-research   200

Series Editor Preface

About the Series

Research and Resources in Language Teaching is a groundbreaking series whose aim is to integrate the latest research in language teaching and learning with innovative classroom practice. The books are written by a partnership of writers who combine research and materials writing skills and experience. Books in the series offer accessible accounts of current research on a particular topic, linked to a wide range of practical and immediately useable classroom activities. Using the series, language educators will be able both to connect research findings directly to their everyday practice through imaginative and practical communicative tasks and to realise the research potential of such tasks in the classroom. We believe the series represents a new departure in language education publishing, bringing together the twin perspectives of research and materials writing, illustrating how research and practice can be combined to provide practical and useable activities for classroom teachers and at the same time encouraging researchers to draw on a body of activities that can guide further research.

About the Books

All the books in the series follow the same organisational principle:

Part I: From Research to Implications

Part I contains an account of current research on the topic in question and outlines its *implications for classroom practice*.

Part II: From Implications to Application

Part II focuses on transforming research outcomes into classroom practice by means of practical, immediately useable activities. Short introductions signpost the path from research into practice.

Part III: From Application to Implementation

Part III contains methodological suggestions for how the activities in Part II could be used in the classroom—for example, different ways in which they could be integrated into the syllabus or applied to different teaching contexts.

Part IV: From Implementation to Research

Part IV returns to research with suggestions for professional development projects and action research, often directly based on the materials in the book. Each book as a whole thus completes the cycle: research into practice and practice back into research.

About This Book

Over the course of their careers language teachers encounter different professional issues, and different teachers experience different levels of motivation and engagement in teaching. This book is not about activities for the language classroom; it is one that is for and about teachers themselves as they pursue their careers. It focuses on teacher development over a lifetime of professional change and engagement. The three authors, all highly experienced in the field of teacher education, draw on research that documents teachers' own perspectives on their professional development and professional lives as the basis for a wide range of activities. It encourages teachers who might be at different points in their profession to explore issues in their careers that are pertinent to where they have come from, where they are now, and where they might go in the future. The activities are designed to help language teachers respond creatively to different needs and themes they identify in their development, to consider the wider implications, and to reflect on the possibilities for researching their own professional situation further.

We hope that you will find the series exciting and above all valuable to your practice and research in language education!

Anne Burns and Jill Hadfield (Series Editors)

Part 1

From Research to Implications

A. Introduction

Whatever the reason you go into teaching—whether it is for love of
the subject, because of family tradition, the intercultural contact with
students, the wish to make a difference, or the job security—and
regardless of whether you aim to stay in teaching for a short time before
doing something else, or you regard teaching as a calling or a plan for
life, things happen to refine and even change those hopes and aims.
Some of us will leave after a while to pursue other career paths; others
may be promoted out of the classroom or burn out on the job; and
others will, sometimes to their own surprise, stay on . . . and on.

It may seem to the individual teacher that the reasons for staying or
leaving are personal ones. You might explain it to yourself (and others)
as due to a family or health situation, or because of changes where
you work, or because you realise you have chosen the wrong job or
have had to cope with too many changes and reforms. Alternatively,
you might find that you love working with young learners or developing
new materials and skills. While recognising these circumstances (as
well as the multitude of others not mentioned here), we three authors
believe that those initial motives for entering English language teaching
do evolve, and the possibility for learning as a teacher in the different
contexts in which you work shapes your professional life, and it can
often influence whether you end up staying or leaving teaching.

We include within teacher learning both the preparation, initial training, and
on-the-job support some new teachers receive as they start their careers
and also the gradual development of knowledge, attitudes, and skills that
happens over time as you teach your way through the years. Teacher
learning is an important factor in turning what can seem, at various points in
your career, a stressful, overly routinised, day job into a varied, stimulating,

renewing, and satisfying form of on-going work. As one of the researchers we include in Part 1, Michael Huberman (1991), observed, "the vast majority of teachers [in his study] express an authentic enthusiasm for their own personal and professional development, which, they feel, has sustained them over the years" (p. 180).

All three of the authors trained as language teachers and have worked in classrooms as language teachers and teacher educators for many years. We have worked with those preparing to become teachers on initial teacher training and with those who are teaching through further teacher education courses. We have been sustained throughout our work by our own personal and professional learning, which has been our 'development over time'. Thus, when thinking about how to approach teacher development for this book, our own longevity in the field suggested we pursue it from the vantage point of time. In this book, we would like to share with you some of what we have learned from research and from our own practice.

Choosing Research That Is 'From—Not About—Teachers'

As we reviewed the major research that relates to the theme of this book, teacher development over time, we realised that two dimensions needed to inform our decisions about what to include in Part 1. Clearly the content is centrally important—the research we selected frames the issues we want to discuss and anchors those issues in careful study of teachers' experiences. However, we were also concerned that the work we chose would represent teachers' professional lives from their own points of view. In other words, the research we included comes *from* the work that teachers do; it is not simply an external view *about* teachers' work. This orientation—that we wanted studies which described teachers' own views of how their work develops through a professional lifespan—is what we mean by the phrase, choosing research that is '*from*—not *about*—teachers'. In terms of research methodology, we wanted to use studies that documented teachers' *own views* of their development over time. These are studies that seek to understand teaching from teachers' perspectives, from an 'emic' or insider's view.

Three Researchers Who Have Studied the Trajectories of Teacher Development

We selected three researchers—Dan Lortie, Michael Huberman, and Amy Tsui—who met these criteria. We refer to them as 'trajectorists' because they each have studied the arc of teachers' understandings of their work over time. The patterns and trajectories these researchers have identified can offer insights into teacher development. We explain a bit about each of them below.

Dan Lortie, a sociologist from the University of Chicago, was one of the first researchers in the early 1970s to conduct a large-scale study of teachers' experiences (Lortie, 1975). His is the first research discussed in this section. **Michael Huberman**, whose work is the second reported in this section (Huberman, 1989), is a Swiss-American researcher who followed on Lortie's impulses in many senses by examining the experiences of Swiss secondary-school teachers to identify possible patterns in how they experience teaching over time. Both Lortie's and Huberman's work could be considered groundbreaking, both in the content of their studies and in the ways in which these studies were conducted. Their work led to broad areas of research into how the conditions of teaching shape teacher learning, and how that learning can be characterised over time. The third researcher, **Amy B. M. Tsui**, represents a different strand. In this section, we draw on her outstanding synthesis of research on expertise and teaching knowledge (Tsui, 2003). In her study, she brings together an impressive amount of research in a coherent way, challenges some of its basic tenets, and uses the data from her study of four teachers to create a clear conceptual model of how expertise develops.

In selecting these researchers, we decided to draw on our different perspectives and to write about them in our individual styles. We hope that you will find it engaging (and not simply a bumpy read). We wanted to remind you, as reader, of our different voices and points of view. We start by explaining what interested us about each of the researchers and why we chose them.

Donald *re. Lortie*: I remember when I first heard about the study *Schoolteacher*. I was teaching in Japan in the early 1980s and attended a workshop on observation and 'breaking the rules' (Fanselow, 1987). We were talking about how we develop our expectations of how to act as teachers, and the presenter brought up what for me was a new idea of teacher socialization. He mentioned the idea of the 'apprenticeship of observation'—the time we spend as students, observing our teachers and participating in their work from 'the other side of the desk'—and how that shaped our expectations of what teachers do and how they behave. He commented, in passing, that the ideas came from a 'great new book . . . *Schoolteacher*, by a sociologist, Dan Lortie'; we should check it out, he said. It slid by me, as a lot of book recommendations do; then almost a decade later, I picked up the book in graduate school. I was amazed by how apt the findings seemed to be. The study captured key issues I was thinking about in how people learn to teach, and gave succinct expression to complex experiences. On a personal level, they spoke to my own experiences as a high school French, and later ELT, teacher (Freeman, 2016). Unlike other studies that come on the scene, and then fade over time, Lortie's ideas have had a durability to them that seems to come from the depth of their connection to teachers' work and experiences. So as we were talking through the research that could anchor this book, I thought immediately of *Schoolteacher*.

Tessa *re. Huberman*: I was editing an article for *The Teacher Trainer* journal in 1991. The piece was written by Jenny Jarvis, then at Warwick University, who was explaining how she tried to make sure that the in-service courses that she ran for teachers from a variety of countries were maximally relevant to their needs. She asked participants to take their time filling out a thought provoking questionnaire before the course. Some of the questions were based on the work of Michael Huberman and she quoted from him, writing about different phases in a teacher's career. His article sounded so interesting that I asked if she could send me a copy. She kindly did. I read it and the related book reporting his team's study and have done so many times since then. I love the work for many reasons. First, for the initial impetuses Huberman gave for undertaking the research project, and that in designing his research he was so on the side of teachers. He writes, "It is worth remembering that the best expert of a given professional trajectory is precisely the person who has followed it" (Huberman, 1991, p. 20).

Then I loved the report for his dry sense of humour. The quotes from the teachers in his study are powerful, too. Most of all, I appreciate the respect he gave the teachers and the care with which he not only navigated the dimensions of age, cohort, psychological and physical maturation, political and social change, historical period, and educational reforms in the work but also consequently warned readers to take his team's work as descriptive and not prescriptive.

Kathleen *re. Tsui*: I first met Amy Tsui when I attended a colloquium on sociocultural perspectives on learning and second language acquisition at the TESOL international conference in 2005 in San Antonio Texas. She presented a paper on young learners and collaborative group work in which she described a seismic shift in her thinking about curriculum from a syllabus-driven, cognitive processing model to an ecological, communities of practice model. I was familiar with this contrast from my own PhD research but was struck by how elegantly and persuasively she illustrated it with two simple sets of questions that teachers might ask themselves in preparing units of work. I later used these questions in an article about curriculum. This clarity of thinking grounded in examples of practice is a hallmark of her book on expertise. Her respect for the complexities of the lives of the four teachers she studied was evident in the way she wrote about their histories, dilemmas, doubts, and successes.

Organisation of Part 1

Having explained what interests us about each of the 'trajectorists', in the next section, 'The Research', we identify and elaborate specific ideas from their work. We end that section with a discussion of more recent research from the *Learning4Teaching* Project, which has studied how teachers in three countries understand the professional development they participated in, what they learned from it, and how they used it in their practice. The *Learning4Teaching* Project was designed and carried out by two of the authors, Freeman and Graves, and a group of colleagues in each of the countries involved. We include this research for two reasons. Like Lortie, Huberman, and Tsui, the studies focus on teachers' perceptions of their learning. The studies are also transnational and large-scale, meaning they bring in perspectives of teachers across three countries, which allows us to consider current issues impacting on professional development in public-sector ELT.

For each of the research studies, we first describe the design, its purpose, the participants, and how it was carried out. We then list and discuss key ideas from the research that can help us to understand teachers' professional development.

In the final section, 'Implications of the Research,' we explore some implications of the key ideas for teacher development. We discuss each researcher in turn, and how their ideas can help us to understand and shape our development as teachers. These implications provide the bridge to Part 2, which provides practical ideas for development over time.

B. The Research: Key Ideas About Teacher Development Over Time

1. Dan Lortie, *Schoolteacher: A Sociological Study* (1975)

In the introduction, we explained the rationale for the research we have chosen to frame the issues in this book: that the work either fomented or synthesised key ideas about teacher development over time, and that methodologically it represented teachers' experiences from their own perspectives. Dan Lortie's *Schoolteacher: A Sociological Study*, first published in 1975, fits these two criteria. The study broke ground in documenting teachers' experiences of teaching and of learning to teach, in their own words. Process-product research, which prevailed at the time, studied how particular teaching processes 'produced' learning outcomes (see Dunkin and Biddle, 1974). In this methodological context, Lortie's study, alongside Philip Jackson's *Life in Classrooms* (1968), sought to chronicle teaching as it was done and experienced by teachers. The sheer scale of qualitative data gathering, combined with the care and complexity of 'grounded' analyses that worked to tease out themes and patterns in teachers' own terms, helped to make Lortie's study an original source for understanding teacher development.

1.1 About the Study: 'Where Teachers and Students Meet'

Lortie begins by explaining the focus of the study:

> It is widely conceded that the core transactions of formal education take place where teachers and students meet. Almost every school practitioner is or was a classroom teacher; teaching is the root status of educational practice . . . Although books and articles instructing teachers on how they should behave are legion, empirical studies of teaching work—and the outlook of those who staff schools—remain rare.
>
> (p. vii)

To examine teachers' experiences, Lortie drew on in-depth interviews—94 in all—that were conducted in "the summer of 1963" (p. 246) in what he called the 'Five Towns' study of schools in New England, in the northeast of the United States. The teachers were chosen deliberately so that respondents fell into what he called "a five-cell sample (with equal numbers in each cell)" (p. 245) as depicted in Table 1.1.

Table 1.1 Lortie's 'five-cell' research design

Teachers drawn from	Ele-mentary schools	Senior high schools	Junior high schools	Ele-mentary schools	Senior high schools
From schools in	"upper income communi-ties"	"upper income commu-nities"	"the middle range"	"lower-income settings"	"lower-income settings"

From Research to Implications

In New England in the 1960s, the 'elementary' schools would likely have included Kindergarten through Grade 5, or possibly Grade 6, while 'junior high' school would likely be Grades 6 or 7 and Grade 8, and 'senior high school' would have been Grades 9 through 12. Within each group, the choices of teachers to interview was random; for instance, "[i]n the upper-income high school cell, 20 names were randomly selected from a container containing the names of all the teachers. In other cells, all teachers were listed alphabetically and selected on the basis of the interval that would produce 20 teachers from the [school] system" (p. 246).

A year later, in 1964, Lortie had the opportunity to survey teachers in Dade County, Florida, USA, in which he included "some items which checked the earlier work done in Five Towns" (p. 246). Here again, the level of care in how the survey was done reflects an acknowledgement of how the conditions of work might shape who responded "Teachers, as well as librarians and administrators . . ., were gathered at 12 locations and filled out the questionnaire during school hours" (p. 246).

The reader may wonder why this level of methodological detail matters. More than 50 years later, it indicates two things: The researcher's commitment to gather data that would document a range of teachers' experiences, and his view that this documentation, while the data and opinions come from individuals, could be seen to be as representative of the breadth of those experiences. In other words, the data was from individuals, but it was meant to capture patterns in their collective experience. Throughout this work, Lortie remained explicit about the goal of the study as gathering and documenting teachers' experiences of their work: "People at work are inclined to dignify and elaborate the significance of the tasks they perform to earn a living . . . Classroom teachers are no exception. It should be helpful, therefore, to examine the form their elaborations take. High ideals are not, after all, without significance in the affairs of men and women" (p. 111).

1.2 Key Ideas

The scope of data-gathering in the *Schoolteacher* study, and the complexity of making sense of it (in an era before computer technology was regularly used in such research), produced a layered and nuanced set of analyses that would be difficult to reduce to a summary. Indeed, any synthesis could run counter to Lortie's commitment to capturing a broad understanding of teachers' experiences. Instead, in this section I have chosen to elaborate five central points from Lortie's analysis: the apprenticeship of observation, relational conditions of teaching, the people-work of teaching, craft pride, and the egg-crate profession/one-step career. These are points that have had an enduring influence on how teacher learning and development are conceptualised and studied.

As analytic ideas, the points share some interesting attributes. Each expresses an aspect of the relational work of teaching (Cohen, 2011): how the individual teacher's work is anchored in various contexts of social interaction—working with students, other teachers, and administrators. Lortie encapsulated each of these complex ideas in a phrase that has taken on a life of its own beyond the study. If you search for the 'apprenticeship of observation', for example, you will find a list of other studies and references that have been spawned by the idea. In this sense, although the points are key findings from the original study, they have become important and have travelled as analytic concepts to shape how we think about teacher development. This dynamism and influence is a hallmark of Lortie's study. Finally, as key ideas from the study expressed in short phrases, the points present views of teacher learning and development that can be applied flexibly across situations and contexts.

1.2.1 The Apprenticeship of Observation

Of the findings from Lortie's study, the phrase 'the apprenticeship of observation' has arguably become the most widely known and cited. He introduces the idea as follows:

> One often overlooks the ways general schooling prepares people for work . . . [P]articipation in school has a special occupational effect on those who move to the other side of the desk. There are ways in which being a student is like serving an apprenticeship in

teaching; students have protracted face-to-face and consequential interactions with established teachers.

(p. 61)

Lortie goes on to quantify and qualify that contact, roughly estimating that "those who teach have normally had sixteen continuous years of contact with teachers and professors." He points out that most young people who grow up in industrialised societies "see teachers at work more than any occupational group". He estimates that students have spent 13,000 hours "in direct contact with classroom teachers by the time they graduate from high school" (p. 61). It is not just the simple fact of protracted contact, he argues, but its qualitative dimension that makes it so central in shaping how those who later become teachers think about and understand the work they do. This apprenticeship is not 'passive observation'. "It is a relationship which has consequences for the students and thus is invested with affect" (p. 61). He describes this stance using the ideas of symbolic interaction theory, that the student 'takes the role' of the teacher "to engage in at least enough empathy to anticipate the teacher's probable reaction to his [sic] behavior" (p. 62). Students "project themselves into their teachers' positions, imagining how the teacher must feel in response to certain student actions and behaviors" (p. 62).

This empathy for teachers forms the basis for our ideas of how the work of teaching 'ought to' work. In other words, the time spent participating as a student lays down a foundation of experience that provides a sort of default option as we are learning to teach. The saying, 'Teachers teach as they were taught, and not as they were taught to teach', encapsulates a rather deterministic view of the professional learning process; while the saying is overly simplistic, it does contain elements of truth. Rather, it is probably fair to say that 'people teach *in relation to* how they themselves were taught'; in other words, they take on certain attitudes and practices from their socialisation as students that resonate with who they are and who they want to be as teachers, and they also reject—or 'teach against'—other dimensions of these experiences.

For many new teachers, this tension between what to emulate from their 'apprenticeship of observation' and what to reject and discard can surface in their assumptions about equity and the abilities of their first students. Ideas about 'who can do what' or, more often, 'why a certain student *can't* do something' are often firmly anchored in our own socialisation in classrooms as students. For instance, young boys who rarely encounter a male teacher may come to think, without reflection, that men don't teach in primary school. In the context of teaching languages, teachers who grow up speaking the language they are teaching do not have the same 'apprenticeship of observation' as do teachers who may have studied the language in school themselves. This difference in experience reinforces a dichotomy between 'native' and 'non-native' speaker which, although it is widespread, is theoretically unsustainable. In fact, a person who is teaching their 'native language'—the language they grew up using outside the classroom—can lack knowledge about how that language 'works' when it is taught as lesson content. They may not have explicit grammatical knowledge or may not be able to explain why certain linguistic constructions function as they do.[1]

Refining these ideas of how students observe teachers and participate in their work, Lortie makes several points. The first has to do with perspective: that a student only sees the teacher from their own particular, individual point of view, whereas a teacher has to see and think about the group of students—as 30 or so individuals that make up the class as a collective. Second, the student's perspective is 'imaginary'. As Lortie puts it, "The student is the 'target' of teacher efforts and sees the teacher front stage and center like an audience viewing a play. Students do not receive invitations to watch the teacher's performance from the wings; they are not privy to the teacher's private intentions and personal reflections on classroom events." "They are, he concludes, witnesses from their own student-oriented perspectives" (p. 62).

The 'apprenticeship of observation' lays out the basis for an experiential foundation for learning to teach. Lortie concludes, "What students learn about teaching, then, is intuitive and imitative rather than explicit and analytical; it is based on individual personalities and not pedagogical principles" (p. 62). This experiential 'apprenticeship' identifies a powerful source of images, attitudes, and reasoning that all contribute to how we work as teachers, starting with our initial preparation. As Lortie puts it, "The mind of the education student [or new teacher] is not a blank awaiting inscription" (p. 66). The durability of this 'apprenticeship of observation' is attributable, at least in part, to the nature of teaching, which the next points speak to.

1.2.2 Instructional Outcomes and Relational Conditions of Teaching

> The complexity of the teacher's classroom situation [is that] control must be maintained, work must be ordered, and the students' interests must be aroused and sustained. These must be met within a group over which the teacher presides.
>
> (p. 152)

In the statement above, Lortie distils what he identifies as the central features of the work of classroom teaching: that teachers must balance 'maintaining control and ordering work' with engaging and supporting 'students' interests' and motivations, and all within the complex social ecology of 'the group'. On one hand, teachers have positional authority to organise what goes on—what we gloss as 'teaching'; on the other, they have to negotiate student interests and engagement—in other words, a teacher cannot compel 'learning'.

He describes this tension, which we often refer to as the challenge of engaging students or as class management, as the interplay between "ultimate instructional results and proximate relational conditions" (p. 117). These instructional results, he says, are usually visible through the curricula, assessments, and teaching standards as 'the ends' teachers are supposed to address. He points out that these relational conditions, which he refers to as 'the means' of teaching, carry their own outcomes that orient teachers' work and often define their sense of success. He identifies three in his analysis: "1) [producing] affection and respect from students; . . . 2) [getting] work out of students; 3) [and] . . . winning student compliance and discipline" (p. 117).

This analysis of how the social interactions between teacher and students—the relational conditions of teaching—shape a teacher's sense of success is probably even more pronounced in the language classroom, where the content—language—depends on 'what goes on inside and between people', to use Stevick's (1976) well-known phrase. Allwright (1996) has noted what he referred to as the 'covert conspiracy' that can characterise language lessons: that as students we must be learning something here since we're all getting along so well. Or to describe this conspiracy using Lortie's terms: the 'relational conditions' in the language classroom come to substitute for 'instructional results', in the minds of teacher and students.

Lortie's 'instructional outcomes and relational conditions', like Allwright's 'covert conspiracy', characterise teaching as fundamentally a matter of balancing demands of the social and the pedagogical aspects, demands that are at times in opposition, often in competition with one another, and always in some sort of tension. Lortie refers to these constant tensions as creating an emotional climate of 'endemic uncertainty', which is the next point. The idea of endemic uncertainty is not necessarily negative for Lortie; rather, it is descriptive. It characterises for him the work that teachers do.

1.2.3 Endemic Uncertainty and the People-Work of Teaching

Lortie refers to teaching as 'people work'. Considering it as a sociologist, as a form of labour, he identifies two, what he calls, 'peculiarities'. Teachers choose to be in the classroom; students (at least those who are children) generally do not. Lortie refers to this as "the *low degree of voluntarism* in the teacher-student relationship" (p. 137, italics added). The two parties are in the classroom to do something together. They share a goal, like learning a language, but as he points out, "neither party brings pre-existing bonds to the relationship" (p. 137). So 'what goes on inside and between people', to use Stevick's phrase, is happening in this social context that is based on participation which is largely involuntary. We often refer to this state of affairs using ideas like 'students who lack motivation' or 'who aren't interested in the class' or 'who are resisting what they need to do.'

Classrooms, particularly language classrooms, call for some degree of cooperation in order to get the work done, a dynamic that Lortie refers to with the great phrase as "the problem of extracting work from immature workers" (p. 137). Unlike other forms of labour, which may be individual, the work in classrooms is generally social. As he puts it, "goals must be met and relationships managed in a group context" (p. 137). In this intensely social context of work, it can be difficult for teachers to know how they are doing: Teaching, Lortie points out, "demands the capacity to work for protracted periods without sure knowledge that one is having any positive effect on students" (p. 144). This adds to the endemic uncertainty of the job; essentially, teachers have to be the judge of how they are doing.

How, then, do we as teachers cope with this uncertainty, with the general lack of agreed-upon ways to measure our performance, to know the kind of job we are doing? In his analysis of teachers' responses, Lortie identifies a process of making do, which he calls 'satisficing', a term he borrows from two organisational theorists of the period, March and Simon (1958). Satisficing is a form of internal evaluation, of negotiation with yourself in which you frame the work as a balancing act between what you need to get done and who you are doing it with, between "accepting X goal achievement and Y relational conditions" (p. 155). If we think about teaching in this way, satisficing means viewing students' learning (both the process and the outcomes) as an interplay between what they need to learn (the 'X goal achievement') and the fabric of social interactions (the 'Y relational conditions') in the classroom.

Let's say you are teaching a class of intermediate-level, secondary school students who are supposed to be completing projects about climate change that they will present and write up. The deadline is next week and some groups are further along than others, having perhaps taken the task more seriously (reflecting the 'degree of voluntarism in the teacher-student relationship' that Lortie noted above). As you circulate among the groups, you are checking where each is with the assignment, which groups will be ready to present the next week, which are behind, and other details. Based on that information, and knowing what is coming next in the curriculum and the schedule, you have a decision to make: Do you hold to the presentation date? Or postpone it? Or work a compromise in which, maybe, you spread the presentations out, giving the groups that are lagging a bit more time? This process of juggling various factors and demands to make a decision is satisficing: It is not negative at all; it is in the very nature of teaching. Thinking about what teachers do from this perspective raises the question of what teachers need to know, the kinds of knowledge they use to negotiate this constant satisficing, and then how this knowledge develops over time.

1.2.4 Craft Pride—A Form of Teacher Knowledge

Schoolteacher is often cited in the educational research community as a study that helped to inaugurate a different view of teacher knowledge. When it was published in the mid-1970s, the study differed quite dramatically from the process-product research of the period that examined teacher behaviours and actions to develop definitions of knowledge and skills from the outside-in. Lortie's was an interview-based study; he focused on the internal dimensions of the work by asking teachers what they thought and what they knew.[2] He characterises this view of teaching knowledge as "marked by the absence of concrete models for emulation, unclear lines of influence, multiple and controversial criteria, ambiguity about assessment timing, and instability in the product" (p. 136). To work with these uncertainties, teachers develop what he calls 'craft pride' which connects them to what they 'find exciting': "the prospect of inducing positive attitudes among their students toward school or toward a particular branch of learning." "They hope", he argues, "that their teaching will produce affective changes" (p. 114). Primary teachers are generally concerned with attitudes towards school; for secondary teachers, the focus shifts to "a particular branch of learning" (p. 114). As a social process and a school subject, language shows up in—and indeed transcends—both arenas.

This tension characterises teaching as a different form of craft knowledge because it cannot be "assessed in terms of a single major purpose"; as he puts it, "the standard of assessment [of teaching] is not unitary" (p. 136). In contrast to "[t]he lawyer [who] wins or loses his [sic] case [or] the engineer's bridge that bears a specified weight or does not . . . Teaching acts are normally assessed according to multiple criteria applied simultaneously" (p. 136). Lortie goes on to give two examples that give face validity to how he describes the tensions in teachers' work[3]: "The teacher who holds the class spellbound may be faulted for inaccuracies of content", he points out. Or "reprimanding a particular child may calm the rest of the students but provoke allegations of inequity from the accused" (p. 136). These tensions bring into focus the interplay of instructional goals and social conditions discussed earlier, and the way teachers have to satisfice their way between the two. It is impossible thus to untangle teachers' craft pride, and the teaching knowledge they draw on, from the social settings of classrooms and schools in which they generate and use that knowledge.

1.2.5 Egg-Crate Profession and the One-Step Career

This is the last in this summary of Lortie's points. As teaching knowledge, teachers' craft pride develops under a peculiar set of organisational circumstances. "Teachers spend most of their working hours outside the view of other adults" (p. 149), which leads Lortie to refer to teaching as an 'egg-crate profession'[4]. "The isolation of the cellular structure" he writes, "and its attendant privacy", (p. 149) combine with the multiple standards by which the work is judged to make it difficult for teachers to know just how well they are doing. He puts this point rather starkly. The 'egg-crate profession', he says, "reduces the joy [of teaching] . . . [Teachers often therefore] crave reassurance which, for them, [can] only come from superiors or teaching peers" (p. 149). Like water in a hole on a sandy beach, social approval tries to fill the vacuum of contradictory instructional and social goals of teaching. In a sense, since it is almost impossible to do the job right by most public standards, teachers turn to one another for support and judgment of their relative success.

While the phrase 'egg-crate profession' describes teaching from the inside-out, its counterpart, the 'one-step profession', describes the work from the outside-in, as the public sees the job. "Teaching is a relatively unstaged career", Lortie points out; "[t]he main opportunity for making major status gains lies in leaving the classroom" (p. 99). In most careers, individuals maintain their core identity even as they move up in status within the profession; "[a] soldier is still a soldier when he is promoted" (p. 84). In teaching, the job looks essentially the same—publicly at least—from the first day a teacher enters the classroom until they retire.

2. Michael Huberman, *The Lives of Teachers* (1989)

This section examines the work of Michael Huberman, Professor of Education at the University of Geneva, Switzerland, first published in 1989, on the professional career cycles of teachers. Huberman worked in the city and canton of Geneva, Switzerland, in a fairly 'monolithic', 'homogenous' school system with a strong bureaucracy (p. 54). He drew on the classical literature of the human life cycle (see Erikson, 1950; White, 1952) and on the literature dealing specifically with the full professional trajectories of classroom teachers (see Ball & Goodson, 1985, Sikes et al., 1985). He synthesised this literature, evoking central tendencies with respect to the leitmotivs of different phases of teachers' lives and the orders of these phases. In his own study, he refined the models used to date, suggesting we can plot trends in teachers' careers roughly related to the number of years of teaching.

2.1 About the Study: "Several People ... Have Characterised This Research as an 'Insane' Undertaking"

Huberman agreed to some extent with the quote above from some, including members of his team, for the study involved 5 years of work and masses of data. His reply was, however, "[c]ertainly, this is a bit ambitious. You have to love this kind of work to do it" (p. xi).

Between 1982 and 1985, he and his team studied 160 practising secondary teachers in the city and canton of Geneva and the neighbouring canton of Vaud. The group, which included teachers of all subject matters with 5 to 39 years of teaching experience, contained slightly more women than men. The research team interviewed teachers, asking them how they felt about their work. The aim was therefore to gather teachers' views of teaching over time. The interviews, which were spread over two sessions, lasted about five to six hours each. Some questions were open-ended; some more tightly structured; others called for responses to prompts on flash cards and checklists. There resulted from the interview tapes and notes 30 pages of transcribed notes per respondent, complex statistical analyses coupled with qualitative analyses, and 700 pages of technical reports. Certainly an ambitious undertaking!

The teacher informants in the study were asked in ethnographic interviews to review their career trajectories in order to discern key themes and to name them. They were then asked to plot the themes, sequentially if possible, into phases that would capture the flow of their professional experience. There were no constraints: The informants could choose any theme, any sequence, and any configuration of features within the phases they identified. Once the data was in, the researchers compared themes across sub groups such as gender, type of school, number of years teaching, and so on, across the whole sample, comparison of sequences, and career trajectories and trends. Some common itineraries were found across several sub groups.

Huberman admits to two main motives for conducting the study. The first was 'reckless curiosity'! He found the initial research questions irresistible, such as: How did teachers construe their activity at different points in their career? How did teachers view their younger and older colleagues? Are there best years for teaching? Which core features of teaching are gained at which points of the career cycle?

The second reason for the study, Huberman states, was more mischievous. School officials in Geneva, he says, thought they 'knew' which 'types' of teacher grew stale and which didn't, which new instructional materials were not being used in which older teachers' classrooms, and so on, and they made decisions based on these judgments. Huberman suggests that the evidence base for these sorts of pronouncements was very soft: "People work up explanations for social phenomena based on scant, often distorted data" (p. 39). So he wanted to look more systematically at such 'taken for granted' phenomena.

2.2 Key Ideas

Huberman nested the main findings of this study within the construct of career phases or stages from earlier literature. Instead of the three-phase model found in much American literature of the period (training, untenured novice, and veteran), Huberman chose five experience groups. Individuals in them spoke about all the periods they had experienced in their career to date.

Huberman reminds us very carefully that the identification of phases and sequences (sketched in Table 1.2) needs to be handled gingerly. The phases and sequences are descriptive rather than normative. That is, they describe processes that may tend to happen and themes that may come up for some teachers, but they do not dictate what *must* happen for any individual or group. For example, some teachers stabilise early on, some much later and some not at all. Others stabilise early only to destabilise later on. "Career development is a process, not a series of events" (Huberman, 1989, p. 32). He suggests that, instead of applying a rigid, determinist set of labels and boxes, we assign a supple, suggestive status to each 'phase' because, although it may characterise a large number of teachers, it will never describe everyone.

Table 1.2 Huberman's model of themes in teachers' career cycle

Years of Teaching	Themes/Phases
Career entry: 1–3 years	"Easy or Painful Beginnings" 'Survival/Discovery'
4–6 years	"Stabilisation"
7–18 years	"Experimentation/Activism" "Self-Doubt"
19–30 years	"Serenity / Relational Distance / Conservatism"
31–40 years	"Disengagement: Serene or Bitter"

From Research to Implications

2.2.1 Themes in Different Career Stages

The insights gained from the Swiss study, and from Huberman's synthesis of previous survey literature, are many and rich, and they arise directly from the experiences, memories, and words of the teacher informants. For instance, Huberman noted that a theme of 'survival' recurs in many interviews of teachers who are in the phase of career entry (1 to 3 years in the job). "The survival theme has to do with reality-shock . . . (as the new teacher confronts) . . . the complexity and simultaneity of instructional management . . ." (p. 33). Many readers will recognise this theme! Perhaps it's the discrepancy between the theories taught in our teacher training programme contrasting with real life in the classroom that shocks us. Perhaps it's the sheer number of hours spent planning and preparing for each 45-minute lesson! Typical preoccupations of a starter teacher might then be 'Am I up to this? 'Can I cope?'

The more optimistic 'discovery' theme, also mentioned by teachers in the same, career-entry stage, points up the pleasure a new teacher might find in having their own pupils, their own classroom; being a colleague among peers, a member of the education guild or teachers' union, and able to walk into the room marked 'Teachers' Room' without having to knock!

The theme of 'stabilisation', which emerges among teachers between 4 and 6 years in the classroom, may entail a definite commitment to the career of teaching and the concomitant giving up of other occupational possibilities such as journalism or the theatre. By this time, teachers may well have got a number of routines under their belts, adding to them, refining them, and so developing their own congenial style and sense of ease in the classroom. This is already very far from the outsider's static view of a teacher at work as one who simply does the same thing over and over for years on end.

The theme of 'experimentation', mentioned by teachers in the next phase of 7 to 18 years, relates to teachers' efforts to increase their impact with a flurry of small scale experiments, trying out different materials, different pupil groupings and other forms of 'pedagogical

20

tinkering' (p. 34). On the other hand, around this time, teachers may also feel 'the stale breath of routine' for the first time. A period of self-doubt occurred for some teachers in the study, either at a fleeting superficial level, giving a feeling of slight monotony or disenchantment or, more fully, as teachers thought seriously of leaving the profession.

For those of us in the business of language teaching nowadays, 18 years may already seem a long time to be in a classroom! Teaching is, perhaps for us, and perhaps for younger people, not always a life-long career. However, when Huberman was writing, there was a very stable, long-term system of employment for teachers in the Geneva and Vaud cantons. His study thus continues to report on the later stages of teachers' life cycles.

Around the 19–30 years mark, some teachers in the study came up with the theme of 'serenity', a phase characterised by slightly more mechanical yet more self-accepting work, 'no more whipping myself for not being perfect'. Increased feelings of serenity sometimes went hand in hand with greater relational distance vis a vis pupils as they stay 'relentlessly young' while an individual teacher ages. Teachers with this number of years of active service sometimes bring up a theme of 'caution or conservatism'. This is where energy lessens, and pupils are perhaps bemoaned as being less disciplined and younger teachers as less committed than they used to be, in a mood of, as my choral conductor says, 'The older I get, the better I was!' But this theme does not emerge universally. Many teachers stated that they had remained energetic, open, committed, and optimistic. In fact, the theme of conservatism only emerges in this study around one age cohort of 19–30 years and only after many years of learning and refining routines, experimenting inside the classroom, and showing activism in the broader professional community outside the classroom.

No more universal is the bitter feeling of having wasted energy over many years of teaching that sadly does occur for some. All those years, all that preparation, all that marking, and for what? Did students really learn as much as I wanted them to? All those staff meetings, all those reforms and those pendulum swings in pedagogical fashion! Only to come full circle again! There may, according to the literature and the study, come a gradual 'disinvestment' towards the end of a professional career. The job is done but more swiftly, with no overtime. No more student outings. No more ambitious class projects. The tone of this may be largely positive, however, as it often means a parallel engagement in other things such as family or hobbies and in more reflection on the work of teaching.

2.2.2 Sequences in the Themes

The research team next drew out common sequences of themes from different sub groups, sequences such as 'harmony recovered'. This was a sequence experienced by teachers who had had an uncomfortable or painful beginning to their career, but who then stabilised, finding their feet well enough to enjoy some classroom experimentation. Another example, called in the study Stabilisation to Reassessment, describes the process experienced by teachers who, confident in their routines and class control, then hit a period of self-doubt. This period might have led to resolution and the finding of a 'second wind' for teaching but, equally, might have remained unresolved, the teacher forever feeling less than satisfied in their work, yet feeling that it is a bit late to try another career.

The team also examined whether themes raised by teachers in the later phases of teaching could be predicted from earlier ones. For example, could cases of either 'career disenchantment' or 'satisfaction' be predicted from earlier themes? The few early predictors that did emerge are suggestive, especially for this book. One factor that seemed to point to professional satisfaction was the value placed on relationships with students. Another was having areas of satisfaction outside school which permitted a teacher to relativise problems at work and view them as only one part of their lives.

2.2.3 'Pedagogical Tinkering'

Another factor that seemed to point to professional satisfaction was the engagement of teachers in classroom experimentation. Huberman (1989) writes,

Teachers who steered clear of reforms or other multiple-classroom innovations but who invested consistently in classroom-level experiments . . . what they called 'tinkering' with new materials, different pupil groupings, small changes in grading systems . . . were more likely to be satisfied later on in their careers than most others and far more likely than peers who had been heavily involved in school-wide or district-wide projects . . .

(p. 50–51)

So 'pedagogical tinkering' (which might at first have sounded a rather belittling or pejorative term), together with an early concern for instructional efficiency, laying down effective practice into routines, getting materials right for most situations, for example, was one of the strongest predictors of later feelings of career satisfaction. As Huberman (1991) explains, "[t]ending one's own private garden, pedagogically speaking, seems to have more pay-off in the long haul than land reform, although the latter is perceived as stimulating and enriching while it's happening" (p. 183). Here we have a recognition of the importance, for teachers, of experimenting and learning within a school atmosphere that supports this.

3. Amy B. M. Tsui, *Understanding Expertise in Teaching: Case Studies of ESL Teachers* (2003)

Amy Tsui's book, *Understanding Expertise in Teaching: Case Studies of ESL Teachers*, published in 2003, grew out of her interest in what makes expert teachers 'expert' and how they become so. Her goal was to both define expertise and to understand how it is achieved. She describes expertise in the following way:

When we say people are experts in their profession, we expect them to possess certain qualities, such as being very knowledgeable in their field; being able to engage in skilful practices; and being able to make accurate diagnoses, insightful analyses and the right decisions, often within a very short period of time. However, what exactly constitutes that expertise is something that is not yet fully understood.

(p. 1)

3.1 About the Study: "What Exactly Constitutes Expertise?"

Tsui's interest in 'what exactly constitutes expertise' led her to frame her study around three questions (p. 3):

1.   What are the *critical* differences between expert and novice teachers?

2.   How does a teacher become an expert teacher? What are the phases that he or she goes through in the process of acquiring expertise?

3.   What are the factors that shape the development of expertise?

The first question concerns how to define expertise; the second and third, how expertise is acquired. In defining expertise, she drew on the research of Berliner (1992, 1994, 1995) and Bereiter and Scardamalia (1993), among others, to make a distinction between 'novice', 'experienced non-experts', and 'expert' teachers. 'Expert' teachers are always experienced teachers, but experienced teachers are not necessarily 'experts'. Tsui writes that, according to Bereiter and Scardamalia, "experts keep extending the upper edge of their competence by setting themselves very high standards and working very hard to reach these standards" (p. 21). The difference between expertise and experience is important because she describes *critical* differences as those that are "indicators of expertise, not just experience" (p. 245). In order to investigate the three questions, she researched the practice of four ESL teachers at various points in their careers. She used what she calls a 'case study approach', focusing on the way each of the teachers "relate to their specific contexts of work, how they make sense of their work as a teacher, and how their knowledge, perceptions, and understanding of their work develop over time" (p. 67).

Tsui's work is similar to Lortie's and Huberman's in that it focuses on teachers and how differences in their identity develop over time, and she uses their own words and perspectives as the basis for analysis. Her study differs from the other two in that she gathered data through intensive direct observation of the teachers in their classrooms as well as interviews with them and examination of teaching artefacts. Her aim, as she puts it, was to provide a "rich and thick description" (p. 67) of these teachers' lives.

Tsui's study also differs from Lortie and Huberman in that she focused on teachers of one subject, English as a foreign language, in one secondary school in Hong Kong. An important tenet of her work is that practise cannot be understood separately from the context in which it is enacted. The practice of teaching is highly situated and responsive to a particular context. By studying same subject teachers in one school, she could reduce possible differences because of subject matter or educational context and thus make differences (and similarities) more salient.

The study would not have been possible without the participation of an expert teacher, whom Tsui calls 'Marina'. Marina was a secondary school teacher of English in Hong Kong. She had been Tsui's student in an in-service teacher education programme and was her MA student at the time of the study. Tsui had been impressed with her outstanding performance in the programme both in theoretical courses and in her practicum, which Tsui supervised. At the time of the study, Marina was in her eighth year of teaching. In addition to teaching English, she was the chair of the English panel (department head in the US, or head teacher in the UK) and thus responsible for oversight of all English classes at the school. In addition to her experience and the way she had developed her competence through professional development and increasing professional responsibilities, Marina was identified as an expert teacher based on highly positive comments from her principal, from her course tutors, colleagues, and students.

Tsui spent three months, from the start of the school year, observing and recording every one of Marina's S2 (Grade 8, age 12) classes. This enabled her to observe Marina teach two complete units in their scheme of work. A unit included work with all four language skills, grammar, vocabulary, and other aspects of language learning the teacher deemed important. Tsui interviewed Marina regularly each week. She also interviewed Marina's students, and she examined Marina's lesson plans, lesson materials, and students' work.

To examine critical differences between 'expert', 'novice', and 'experienced non-experts', Tsui invited three other teachers in the same school with varying years of experience and levels of competence to participate in the study. She observed each of them over a period of a month in which they completed most of a unit from their scheme of work. Two of these teachers had 5 years of teaching experience, while the other was a novice, in her second year of teaching. In addition to observations, Tsui interviewed each teacher regularly and examined teaching artefacts, as she did with Marina; however, she did not interview their students.

In order to discern critical differences between Marina and the other teachers and to identify the factors that contributed to Marina's development of expertise, Tsui focused on three areas in her data analysis:

1) Their professional development—how they came to be teachers and their history of teaching—the different stages of development they had experienced.

2) How they related to their specific contexts of work.

3) The extent to which they were able to theorise the knowledge generated by their personal practical experience as a teacher, and to 'practicalise' theoretical knowledge.

3.2 Key Ideas

The key ideas from Tsui's research are linked to her research questions. One of those questions concerned the teacher's developmental path— how a teacher becomes a teacher, the stages of her development, and how, over time, she makes use of the affordances of her context. Another question explored what she called 'critical' differences between an expert teacher and an experienced non-expert or novice teacher. These differences manifested themselves in how the expert teacher used her knowledge in integrated ways in her practice and how she related to her context. The third question addressed the factors that shaped the development of expertise. She found that expertise is developed through experimentation and pushing the boundaries of one's knowledge.

3.2.1 Teachers' Different Developmental Paths

As she explored their histories as teachers, Tsui found similarities at the beginning stages of their careers. All four teachers reported being overwhelmed in their first year of teaching because of the many demands of the classroom. In that sense, they were experiencing a typical 'survival' stage as they learned to cope with the multifaceted nature of teaching, a stage Huberman amply describes. The three experienced teachers all went through periods of 'self-doubt', asking themselves if teaching was the right choice of career. Their first years were particularly challenging because they started with no formal professional preparation as teachers. For this reason, their educational backgrounds as students (what Lortie called their 'apprenticeships of observation'), their family backgrounds, their life experiences—all played a role in how each person figured out how to be a teacher.

However, despite working in the same school context, their paths diverged after a few years. Tsui refers to the work of Huberman in describing the paths the teachers followed. Marina and Eva, one of the teachers with 5 years of experience, moved out of the phase of 'self-doubt' and into the phase Huberman called 'stabilisation', in which they gained confidence. Huberman points out that novice teachers in a supportive environment are better able to move into the stabilisation phase. Marina and Eva used the supportive environment of their school and were able to negotiate the types of classroom management, discipline issues, and lesson delivery that novices typically confront. On the other hand, Ching, the other teacher with 5 years of experience, was unable to feel this sense of stabilisation and continued to experience teaching as an up and down 'roller coaster'.

When Marina and Eva encountered difficulties in teaching, they experimented and explored different ways of doing things, akin to Huberman's idea of 'tinkering'. Both were able to problematise aspects of their teaching and to use reflection to reframe their understanding of their work and their roles. However, Marina's history differed from Eva's (and Ching's) in one important way: in her fourth year teaching,

Marina was accepted into a two-year Professional Certificate in Education (PCEd). The course helped her to understand why aspects of her practice were successful, and gave her theoretical tools to use in changing her practice. Tsui calls this process 'practicalising theoretical knowledge' (p. 257). While Eva could draw on 'personal practical knowledge' (Clandinin, 1986; Elbaz, 1983), when Marina experimented, she could also draw on theoretical disciplinary knowledge, which Eva did not have. For example, Marina and Eva both used group work. Marina initially used group work as a way to get students to talk. In her PCEd program, Marina learned that group work should have a purpose that can only be accomplished in a group, not something that can be done individually. She came to understand that negotiation of meaning was an important aspect of group work and that collaboration should result in output to be shared with others. Group work in Marina's class thus integrated purpose, collaboration, and outcome. Eva also used group work to get students to participate and work collaboratively. However, the group work was often work that could be done individually and did not always require students to negotiate meaning for a learning outcome. Ching only used group work occasionally because she saw learning as something individual and was concerned that group work did not accurately represent what each individual could do.

3.2.2 'Critical Differences'

By looking at what distinguished Marina's practice from the others, Tsui was able to respond to her first research question about the *critical* differences between expert and novice teachers. She came to the conclusion that there were three dimensions in which critical differences could be identified, as described in Table 1.3: integrating teaching knowledge, relationship to teaching context, and theorising and practicalising.

INTEGRATING TEACHING KNOWLEDGE

Tsui found that as an expert teacher, Marina had a richer and more elaborate knowledge-base than the other teachers in the study, and that she integrated that knowledge into her practice, seamlessly interweaving

Table 1.3 Tsui's critical differences that characterise expert teachers

Integrating Teaching Knowledge	How teachers relate to the act of teaching and the extent to which they integrate or dichotomise the various aspects of teaching knowledge in the teaching act.
Relationship to Teaching Context	How teachers relate to their specific contexts of work.
Theorising and Practicalising	How and to what extent teachers are able to theorise the knowledge generated by their personal practical teaching experience and to 'practicalise' theoretical knowledge.

her understanding of subject-matter, teaching strategies, students, and school context (p. 250–251). This way of working was evident even on her first day of class, in which she introduced classroom routines by introducing herself using adjectives that described her personality (*hard working, punctual, talkative*). Through the discussion of their meaning, she was able to make it clear that *punctuality* was a requirement, *hard work* expected, and that *talkative* meant talking in English. She followed this with an activity in which students chose three adjectives (consulting a dictionary if needed) to describe themselves and wrote them in a vocabulary notebook. This step was followed by pair work, in which the students introduced themselves to each other and explained why they had chosen the adjectives. The layering and integration of instructional objectives (descriptive adjectives) with classroom management (teacher expectations), meaningful work (choosing three adjectives), and student collaboration (interviews) was evident in this and other classes Tsui observed.

In contrast, the other teachers tended to dichotomise or separate areas such as instructional objectives from student interest or engagement. These teachers might, for example, have an activity in which the students enjoyed themselves, but which did not result in language learning. For example, Eva considered her students to be 'successful' in a writing task if they could express their ideals and values, even if their writing did not demonstrate the skills taught.

RELATIONSHIP TO TEACHING CONTEXT

In terms of the second dimension—how teachers relate to their specific contexts of work—Tsui points out that studies of teacher expertise such as Shulman's (1986) conceptualisation of pedagogical content knowledge neglected to account for the relationship between a teacher's knowledge and her teaching context. Drawing on Lave and Wenger's (1991) work on situated learning, Tsui describes the relationship as dialectal. On the one hand, the context—the students, the curriculum, the materials—constrains or determines what a teacher can do. On the other hand, a teacher can identify possibilities offered by the context to shape her teaching. An expert teacher is able to see both the possibilities and constraints of the context and find ways to use the possibilities and overcome the constraints in order to achieve her or his instructional purposes.

For example, Marina understood that her students, who were from working class backgrounds, would not hear or use English outside of school and that the role of English in Hong Kong meant that their success in English would be an important determiner for their future. She determined to create an 'English-rich' environment in the classroom, using realia and authentic texts, exhibiting students' English work on the bulletin board and requiring students to use only English. She also connected the students to English outside of the classroom by giving them literacy tasks such as identifying the English instructions on supermarket products. She made use of external resources, such as adopting the extensive reading programme when it was offered by the local education authority.

Eva also used an English-only policy in order to promote an English-rich classroom. However, she did not appear to make connections to the wider world of the students or to create other English opportunities for them. She also enforced the rule with a penalty system, thus casting it as an obligation rather than an opportunity. The novice teacher had the same policy, but did not enforce it because she was still learning how to get students to obey class rules. The other experienced teacher, Ching, did not use the policy because she felt her students had too much difficulty switching from Chinese to English, so she focused on her own communication with them, thus limiting their possibilities.

Tsui notes that two things made Marina different from the other three teachers in the study in the way she related to the context. First, she recognised the constraints of the context and "actively shaped her context of work by transcending those constraints" (p. 256). Second, she responded to the context not in discrete and disconnected ways, but in a coherent way in which it was evident that she could see both the forest (the overall picture) and the trees (the parts that made up the picture).

'THEORISING' AND 'PRACTICALISING'
The third dimension of expertise Tsui identified is the ability to 'theorise' practical knowledge and 'praticalise' theoretical knowledge. Tsui defines the former as being able to reflect on what one knows and does in order to understand it, to question it, and, if needed, to reshape it, while the second involves being able to take 'formal' concepts and figure out how they can shape one's practice. Expert teachers, Tsui argues, do both. She describes how, over time, Marina grappled with the balance between having a disciplined classroom and also having a classroom in which students enjoyed themselves. As a novice, Marina describes her struggle to maintain strict discipline and how she achieved this goal by being a very strict teacher. She was not entirely happy with the results because "excellent classroom discipline was achieved at the expense of making learning enjoyable" (p. 258). Two critical incidents in which she penalised students for poor work led her to realise that by not being lenient she had forestalled a chance for them to improve. She describes a shift from seeing rules and discipline from her point of view to being able to see them from the students' point of view. Over time, this

allowed her to distinguish between noisy 'off task' classroom behaviour, which detracted from the lesson, and noisy 'on task' behaviour that contributed to it. Her classes became more lively and she established a warmer rapport with her students to the extent that they felt comfortable confiding in her about their problems.

Tsui contrasts Marina's process with one of the experienced teachers, Ching, who had continual difficulty establishing rapport with her students and attributed it to factors such as personality, authority, or the particular group of students. Unlike Marina, who was able to consider a host of factors in describing the problem and find ways to reframe it, as a 'non-expert experienced teacher', Ching sought external reasons over which she felt she had no control. Professional training, Tsui found, also helped Marina to theorise practical knowledge and to understand why something she did was successful. For example, in her practice she tried to use materials that were interesting and relevant to her students. Formal training helped her to understand the "theoretical rationale for using authentic texts" and enabled her to "critique the English that was used in textbooks" (p. 260).

Marina also 'practicalised theoretical knowledge', meaning she took formal concepts learned in her courses and figured out how to put them into practice. For example, the concept that the aim of group work is for all members to contribute towards an outcome, not simply to have a chance to talk, led Marina to change the way she designed group work, so that it became more integrated with her objectives. Another example was the concept that a leader is an agent of change. As chair of the English panel at her school, Marina saw her role as an administrator and not at first as a change agent. Once she took the idea on board, however, she began to identify areas in which teaching and learning could be improved, which led her to implement process writing in the curriculum, a project which is described below.

3.2.3 Experimenting, Problematising, and Distributed Expertise

How do teachers develop in the three dimensions of teaching knowledge, relationship to context, and negotiating the relationship between theory and practice? Tsui suggests that the answer lies in the kinds of experimentation they do. Citing Huberman's finding that classroom level experimentation gives teachers career satisfaction, Tsui suggests that "there is something more to experimentation and exploration than career satisfaction" (p. 267). She argues that experimentation is a process of knowledge renewal that widens the knowledge-base that a teacher can draw on and that this knowledge growth is vital to the development of expertise. The process involves not only drawing on practical knowledge, but also using formal knowledge and making it practical. For any teacher, including experts like Marina, this experimentation happens at the classroom level. Expert teachers, however, can choose to extend their influence beyond the classroom. Marina had long been dissatisfied with how writing was taught. Typically students wrote compositions on assigned topics. These written products were painstakingly corrected by the teacher, and students were asked to make certain corrections. Marina and the teachers agreed it was ineffective—the teachers spent an inordinate amount of time correcting the papers with little improvement in the students' work. In a refresher course Marina had read about process writing. The multiple drafting and refining process it involved made sense to her, although she had no practical experience teaching writing in this way. In her capacity as English panel Chair, Marina decided to introduce process writing into the curriculum. She introduced it in a gradual way that involved the teachers and enlisted their support in evaluating and adapting it to the context.

The implementation of process writing is, in itself, an example that blends her practical knowledge with the theoretical. She identified the need because of current dissatisfaction with how writing was taught. She wanted the students to be able to improve their writing. In this sense, she theorised practical knowledge—she stood back from her experience to analyse it and identify problems. She decided to implement a process writing approach, without having any direct experience of it, as she had not used it herself. In this sense, she undertook to practicalise theoretical knowledge.

Tsui also argued that experts are not content with the status-quo. For example, once Marina had achieved a disciplined classroom, she still felt that there was more that she needed to accomplish. She was able to problematise the seemingly disciplined classroom in order to get at a deeper or wider understanding of how to create enjoyable, productive learning experiences for students. Through conscious deliberation and reflection, she was able to 'reframe' her understanding of the kind of classroom she wanted, thus theorising her practical knowledge. This ability to problematise one's practice and to reframe it in productive ways are characteristics of an expert teacher.

Expert teachers not only respond to challenges, but look for them. Tsui cites the work of Bereiter and Scardamalia (1993) in describing these challenges as ones that enable teachers to work at the edge of their competence. Experts tackle problems that push their limits so that they can increase their expertise; they seek challenges that extend their capabilities. In contrast, non-experts tackle problems that are well within their competence. Marina's implementation of process writing is a clear example of taking on a challenge that was at the edge of her competence as she had no direct experience of it and had to find appropriate materials and feel her way with the teachers. Tsui cautions that challenges should not be beyond one's competence and that experts recognise that there are problems that are beyond what they can address.

Tsui ends her analysis by describing the ways in which expertise is both 'multiple' and 'distributed'. It is multiple in the sense that there are many types of expertise within a profession and one person cannot be expert at everything. This is why, when teachers tackle a new subject area or teach a different group of students, they become novices again. Distributed expertise is closely related to the idea of multiple expertise. In any organisation like a school, different people have different kinds of expertise in order to make the organisation function. In that sense, expertise is social, distributed among the different people in the organisation. Experts recognise that expertise is multiple and that there are limitations to their individual knowledge. They recognise that expertise is distributed and that others have knowledge they do not. They purposefully draw on or make use of these different sources of knowledge. Marina, for example, continually sought support from her principal and other teachers. She enrolled in educational courses that introduced her to new 'discourse communities' and new ways of thinking about her practice. By collaborating with others and participating in different discourse communities, she was able to expand her horizons and deepen her practice. In this respect, collaboration among people is important for the development of individual and group expertise.

Tsui's description of how expertise develops distils the essence of her study:

> [T]he development of expertise in teaching is a continuous and dynamic process in which knowledge and competence develop in previous stages and form the basis for further development. It is also a process in which highly competent teachers constantly set new goals for themselves and accept new challenges. In the process of achieving those goals and meeting these challenges, they gain new insights. It is in the process of constantly gaining new competence that expertise is developed.
>
> (p. 7)

4. The *Learning4Teaching* Project

The *Learning4Teaching* Project is a group of national studies, led by Freeman and Graves with local research collaboration, to examine public-sector ELT teachers' learning from professional development in three countries (Freeman & Graves, 2013; Freeman et al., 2017). These studies share two fundamental characteristics with the research we have discussed thus far in this section. First, the researchers took seriously how teachers view their own learning, and did so by adopting an emic (insiders') perspective to identify how teachers understand their own development. Second, they studied that development over time. Similarly, rather than taking a single snapshot of professional development at one moment in time, Lortie, Huberman, and Tsui each examined how professional learning unfolded and came to make sense to teachers through time across their careers. The *Learning4Teaching* Project research shares and indeed expands on these two characteristics of teachers' emic perspectives over time.

4.1 About the Studies

The Project's premise is that although English language teaching is among (if not) the largest public-sector expenditure that many national governments make in professional development (Isoré, 2009; also e.g. Wang, 2007), how teachers participate and learn from what is offered is rarely studied, and not at scale. ('Scale' here refers to how the professional development, in this case, works throughout the national educational system.) The Project's large-scale phenomenographic research investigates how teachers make sense of professional development available to them as learning opportunities in their national education systems. Studies were conducted in three countries: Chile, Turkey, and Qatar. Each study involved assembling data on the professional development opportunities available to a national sample of the public-sector ELT teaching force. Researchers examined how teachers perceived those opportunities—what they said they learned from the professional development events they attended—and how they reported using what they learned in their classrooms.

Table 1.4 The design of the *Learning4Teaching* Project

	Professional learning→	Teacher participation→		Classroom use
PREMISE	A given professional development activity offers an opportunity to learn	Participating and making sense of an opportunity to learn influences	Individual uptake of ideas and practices, which influences	Using the ideas and practices in the classroom
RESEARCH STUDY	STUDY #1 Inventory of opportunities from providers	STUDY #2 National survey of public-sector ELT teachers	STUDY #3 Teaching logs from subset teachers who completed the survey	STUDY #4 Observation of subset of teachers from logs

Each national investigation involved a sequence of three studies: 1) a national inventory of professional development, 2) a national survey of teachers' experiences, which were followed by 3) teaching logs. Classroom observations were also conducted in some contexts. Table 1.4 summarises the sequenced design of the four studies in each country.

This sequence of Project studies is designed to probe a different view of the possible relationship between professional development, teacher learning, and classroom teaching, as the 'premises' in the top row of Table 1.4 explain. Generally, professional development is seen as 'causing' changes and improvements in classroom practice; however, this view overlooks the complexities of how teachers make sense of professional development opportunities as they transform what they take from these events into usable knowledge in their teaching.

'Causal' Views of Professional Development

In focusing specifically on teachers' experiences, the *Learning4Teaching* Project differs in important ways from general views of how professional development is supposed to influence what teachers do in teaching. The usual logic is often described as a four-step process which leads from the professional development event, through the teacher, to the classroom. This "core theory of action for professional development", one prominent researcher argues, "would likely follow these steps:

1. Teachers experience effective professional development.

2. The professional development increases teachers' knowledge and skills and/or changes their attitudes and beliefs.

3. Teachers use their new knowledge and skills, attitudes, and beliefs to improve the content of their instruction or their approach to pedagogy, or both.

4. The instructional changes foster increased student learning."

(Desimone, 2009, p. 184)

As this 'path model' (Figure 1.1) illustrates, the central premise is that professional development input 'changes' teachers' knowledge and skills, which in turn 'changes' what they do when they teach, which then 'results' in increased student learning.

At its most basic level, the connection is supposed to be one of cause and effect, in which teachers are one element in the chain from professional development input to classroom output, as the arrows in Figure 1.1 suggest. Perhaps more problematic, this causal chain portrays the teachers' inner worlds of thinking and knowing (the second box) as distinct and separable from the public world of their actions in classroom instruction (the third box). In contrast, the conceptual framework of the *Learning4Teaching* Project (Table 1.4) focuses on how teacher learning has to involve sorting through the professional development opportunities, which process can lead them to take up ideas and activities that make sense to them to use in their teaching.

To investigate this premise of sense-making, the *Learning4Teaching* Project has focused on three countries, each of which presents a distinct national environment for English language teaching. The three countries were selected to create a useful set of contrasts among national teaching environments:

- **Chile** has had a continuous national policy, for now over a decade, called 'English Opens Doors' that actively promotes English language

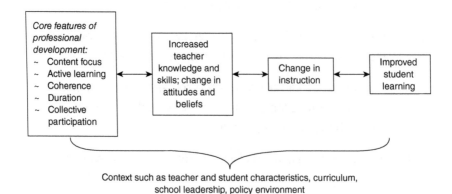

Context such as teacher and student characteristics, curriculum, school leadership, policy environment

Figure 1.1 "Proposed core conceptual framework for studying the effects of professional development on teachers and students" (Desimone, 2009, p. 185)

learning and teaching. We have called this a *policy-oriented* national environment for ELT.

- **Turkey** has a national ELT environment which we called *socially market-oriented*, meaning that learning English is closely tied to expanding economic opportunities and professional advancement.

- **Qatar** is a national environment in which the role of English is in flux. At the time of the study in 2017, 80% of Qatar's population came from five countries: India, Nepal, Qatar, Bangladesh, and Egypt, only two of them Arabic-speaking (Snoj, 2017). This 'minority-majority' language dynamic creates a context for ELT in which English plays the role of *lingua-franca* within national life. We call this a *lingua-franca oriented* context.

In choosing countries with distinct national ELT teaching environments, the assumption, which has been borne out by research in the United States (Coburn, 2005; Coburn & Stein, 2006; Cohen et al., 2009; Spillane, 1996), is that national policies contribute in shaping teachers' views of what matters in teaching and learning.

4.2 Key Ideas

To understand their experiences, the Project surveyed public-sector ELT teachers about their professional development during a 3-year period.[5] Their responses, summarised in Table 1.5, provided a broad look at how teachers in each national environment experience professional development and the sense they make of it.

In all three countries, over 90% of the respondents in each country reported being able to use what they had learned in the professional development in some way, which suggests how valuable they see these opportunities as being. While one might assume this finding suggests that the professional development offered was highly relevant, we think instead that the finding shows the powerful nature of professional learning: that teachers were reporting they were able to find applicability in what they had experienced in these events.

From Research to Implications

Table 1.5 National surveys in the *Learning4Teaching* Project

	CHILE	TURKEY	QATAR
Number of public-sector ELT teachers responding to national survey	1101[a]	2960[b]	661
% of public-sector ELT teachers (estimated)	(45–54%)	(~15%)	(~66%)
Reported professional development events	2305	4119	2038
Subset (# of teachers) who completed daily teaching logs	132	106	54

Note: [a]In Chile, the survey was sent in two waves to 1,101 teachers, with response rates of 45% and 54%.
[b]In Turkey, due to the size of the public-sector ELT teaching force—some 43,000 teachers—a stratified geographic sampling procedure was used. Two cities in each of the eight administrative regions were selected to survey, one a major population centre and the other a smaller city. In making these selections, we endeavoured to include cities that were not in close geographical proximity to each other. Through this stratified sampling distribution, 2,960 teachers responded, with a national response rate of approximately 15%.

Analysis of the qualitative survey data started with what teachers said the professional development was about. It is important to note that the survey asked open-ended questions about the topic and learning from the professional development event, and teachers could respond in the national language or in English. In analysing the responses, the aim was to examine the degree to which there might be some perceived common focus in what was offered. However, different levels of coherence surfaced through this analysis. In Chile, for example, teachers reported about a third of the professional development events were focused on language competence, 20% were about methodology, and a third combined language and methodology, while the remaining approximately 10% were not directly related to ELT. Their perceptions seemed to bear out the government's policy focus on professional development that improved English language skills and teaching methodology. In contrast, in Turkey, the focus seemed less clear: Teachers described about half the professional development in general terms—for example, 'English language teaching methods and techniques' ('İngilizce dersi öğretim programı yöntem ve teknikleri')—while they said 40% of events addressed a range of specific topics (e.g. 'Developing four skills in language teaching—speaking, listening, reading, writing'), and again about 10% was not ELT-related. Similarly in Qatar, teachers reported on 2038 professional development events, of which they said 76% had to do with ELT, while they said 22% were not ELT-related.

4.2.1 Understanding How National Policies Can Create a Vernacular of Purpose

What can be taken from this analysis? First, teachers are not defining professional development in a vacuum; national environments of policies and preferred practices contribute to how they are perceiving what matters in learning and teaching. This point is evident in how the Chilean teachers' perceptions aligned with the specific mandates of the national ELT policy, 'English Opens Doors', to focus on English language improvement and teaching methodology. In both Turkey and Qatar, where the goals of ELT were more generally stated as part of broader educational policies, teachers did not report such a defined focus in the professional development they did. In essence, national policies function as a sort of vernacular language, which provides teachers with ways to make sense of the professional development in which they participate, either voluntarily or required. Beyond this point, however, teachers seem able to find value and usefulness in the professional development they do. In other words, teachers' own agency comes in transforming the professional development they are faced with into something they can use in their individual classrooms. Overall, then, it seems that from the teachers' point of view, participating in professional development is a process of taking what is offered and transforming it into something that can be of use to them in their work. While the topic may or may not be particularly relevant, teachers transform these opportunities for professional learning to their own needs and ends.

4.2.2 Understanding Teachers' Uptake in Professional Learning

To dig into these perceptions involved a closer examination of what teachers said about the professional development events in which they had participated. Here some interesting patterns emerged. These patterns were taken from the open-ended survey responses. Analyses traced connections between how participants *named* and *described* the event, what they reported *learning* from it, and how they said they *used* what they had learned in their teaching. The names and descriptions of the events teachers provided identified the topic, while what they said they learned and how they use it articulated what the project researchers called the 'uptake' from the event. 'Uptake' is defined as how teachers make sense of and use what is available from a professional development event. In this sense, uptake offers a way to look at what teachers say they are learning from professional development.

Uptake is difficult to study on a large scale, however. To do so, teachers need to be able to use their own terms to describe the professional development, and these words need to be categorised to find meaningful common patterns. To this end, teachers' responses on the national surveys were completely open-ended: They could describe the events, and uptake from them, using any language they chose. Thus, one could say that in a conventional sense the possible variety in their responses could be random. To identify patterns in these open responses, project researchers developed a group of categories that were based specifically in the words the teachers chose. They could then trace connections among these categories using procedures of statistical analysis.

Through this work, the process of learning as transforming input into something useable was clearly illustrated. In Turkey, even though participants may have *described* a professional development event in general terms, if they reported *learning* specific things about language or pedagogy, they were more likely to say they had *used* what they learned to address specific aspects of their teaching. For instance, in an event described in general terms as being about 'English language teaching methods and techniques', when teachers said they had learned specific techniques—'how to use four skills (speaking, reading, writing, listening)' or perhaps how to 'direct students to do more project work and increase the diversity of listening tasks', for example—they were more likely to describe specific classroom applications of what they had learned, for example: 'I used different speaking activities and language games in my class' or 'I used different assessment and presentation techniques especially in teaching speaking skills'. The calculation of 'more likely' here compares these answers to random possibility.

In Chile, where the national ELT environment is shaped by the 'English Opens Doors' (Inglés Abre Puertas) policies, when teachers described a professional development event as focused on language—for instance, 'assistencia a un curso de perfeccionamento de ingles' ('attending a course on English improvement')—and they reported learning that focused on their own English, 'Me sirvio para desarollar algunas habilidades como: speaking, listening, reading, grammar'[6] ('It helped me to develop skills such as speaking, listening, reading, grammar'), they were twice as likely to detail specific ways of using what they had learned, by saying, for example, 'by means of new activities'; 'expresion oral' ('oral expression'); 'trabajando con mini-proyectos dentro la sala de clase' ('doing mini-projects in class'). The alignment was similar when Chilean teachers described professional development focused on methodology and they reported learning about mechanics of the language (e.g. 'oral expression'): They were more likely to report specific classroom uses of what they had done.

4.2.3 Understanding Professional Learning Through Teachers' Perceptions

These patterns in teachers' perceptions of their learning offer a large-scale view of how they are making sense of professional development. Some approaches to research might contend that since the data is self-reported, it is somehow less accurate than what might be observable. The *Learning4Teaching* Project challenges this line of argument, however. The assumption that what teachers learn must be observable, and that therefore what they report may be suspect, is based on a one-dimensional view of teaching as behaviour, as doing things in classrooms. But teaching is much more than what is publicly accessible; it involves figuring things out, making sense of what is happening, while responding and intervening to shape the flow of classroom activity (Freeman, 2016). Studying how teachers see and understand what they do is an avenue to opening up this inner world. *Learning4Teaching* researchers would argue that the scale of these reports—data on more than 2000 professional development events in each country—and the breadth of analysis offer a vehicle to understand teachers' sense-making.

Perceptions are powerful; they create a world in which people make sense of what they do. Probing and analysing these worlds permits researchers to enter into how teachers understand their own learning, and to value those emic insights. More fundamentally, these studies point to an important distinction to be made between professional *development* and professional *learning*, as intertwined social processes connected by opportunities to participate (Webster-Wright, 2009). 'Professional development' describes these opportunities as providers see them; 'professional learning' describes how teachers perceive the opportunities. The distinction can be critical to understanding how and why organised teacher learning—in pre- and in-service forms—'works'.

The *Learning4Teaching* research points to how as teachers, we can and do use these formal learning opportunities. We take from the experiences in ways that make sense to us, almost independent of the focus of the professional development. These findings connect to two principal contentions in Huberman's studies: First, that it is more accurate to describe teacher learning not as 'pre-' or 'in-service', but as extending throughout a career. Second, Huberman found that for many teachers, experimentation as a phase in professional learning can lead to career satisfaction. Within this framing, a professional development event could be seen as a forum, and perhaps an impetus, for experimentation. This view connects to the *Learning4Teaching* finding of how teachers transform these events into opportunities for professional learning, or what Tsui refers to as teacher learning through practicalising new knowledge. Overall, these findings underscore that professional development is seen as important by teachers, as evidenced by the scale of responses in these three different countries, and that learning is a process of making sense of these opportunities to make use of the learning in the classroom.

C. Implications of the Research: What We Can Learn About Teacher Development Over Time

In this section, we move between the research and our own work as teachers and trainers. We draw on what we see in these researchers' work to bridge their ideas and our world of teaching so that the ideas may be used as a basis for fruitful teacher learning. As we did in describing the research, we start with Lortie's work, then Huberman, then Tsui, and finally the *Learning4Teaching* Project. In starting with Lortie's work, we begin with someone who studied teaching from the perspective of a sociologist, as the work that teachers do, as viewed from within and outside of the classroom. In this way, the implications are embedded in wider social perceptions of teaching as a job within society. Huberman's study introduces implications for a 'staged' view of teachers' professional lives, a view that examines larger patterns in teaching. Tsui's work introduces implications for how teachers learn and develop teaching knowledge over time and how they understand and use their knowledge in their practice. The *Learning4Teaching* Project examines the ways in which teachers make their own sense of the content of professional development events, not necessarily in the way intended by the providers.

5. Implications of Lortie's Study

As previously noted, Lortie's study, *Schoolteacher*, turned out to be groundbreaking in several ways. It has had implications not only for how we understand teachers' work, but also for how we study it. (The latter, which is discussed more fully in Part 4 of the book, was the notion of asking teachers about their experiences. This research approach created a new perspective on teachers' work and opened up new appreciation for its complexities and competing demands.) In terms of how we understand teachers' work, some of Lortie's observations may strike us as negative or critical of teachers, which is not the point. Rather, in documenting through their own words how these teachers experienced the work, the study gave voice to some of its basic dilemmas. These ideas have implications in three areas:

5.1 How our experiences as students can help us understand the ways we teach (*Apprenticeship of observation*)

5.2 How the work of teaching viewed from the outside (*One-step profession*) contrasts with how we experience it (*Egg-crate profession*)

5.3 How teaching is a balancing act between instructional goals and relational work (*Satisficing*)

5.1 How Our Experiences as Students Can Help Us Understand the Ways We Teach (Apprenticeship of Observation)

Lortie's concept of the 'apprenticeship of observation' is sometimes portrayed as deterministic: that as teachers we are constrained by the kinds of teaching we experienced as students. The saying about the influence of teacher education, discussed in 1.2.1, that 'Teachers teach as they were taught and not as they were taught to teach', reflects this view of professional learning. It is a misreading of Lortie's concept, however. The 'apprenticeship of observation' distils the basic connection between two sets of experiences: those of growing up in school as a student (with all its good and not-so-good aspects), and those of becoming and being a teacher 'on the other side of the desk', as Lortie puts it.

An implication of connecting these experiences is that we do teach *in relation to* how we were taught. Digging into what we liked and didn't like about the instruction we received, what worked and didn't work for us, not just in language classes but across our time as students, can be a very useful exercise. These reflections can (and probably should) extend beyond thinking about the types of teaching activities and materials we experienced—what Lortie categorised as the 'instructional' dimension of those experiences—to include the relational aspects. For instance, if you were a student in mathematics classes in which girls were routinely discouraged, you might form opinions about who can (and can't) do math. While that opinion will likely have a different impact depending on your own gender as well as the teaching in subsequent mathematics classes, it is still residual in your experience. Similarly, if your own language classes emphasised grammatical explanations, that view of class content is bound to influence your own. In teacher preparation or professional development activities, teachers are sometimes asked to examine their experiences as students as a basis for considering new or alternative ways of acting. To some, this type of reflection may seem disconnected from their current responsibilities, but an implication here is that it is not. Understanding our pasts as teachers can provide a prologue to future changes and adjustments in what we make in our teaching. In Lortie's sense, the saying is more accurately put as 'Teachers teach *in relation to* how they were taught, which can *be examined or challenged* through how they were taught to teach.'

5.2 How the Work of Teaching Viewed From the Outside (One-Step Profession) Contrasts With How We Experience It (Egg-Crate Profession)

On one level, this idea is hardly surprising. Many events and practices look and feel different to those who are participating in them than they do to observers. Lortie's two concepts of the 'one-step profession' and the 'egg-crate profession' locate this idea of perspective in the dynamics of teaching specifically. In one sense, teaching is everyone's business. Members of the general public, who have been students themselves, often assume they know what classroom teaching is and understand how to do (or improve) it. The level of political discourse in many countries about education and schools reflects this public interest—and assumed expertise—in what teachers do. Experience in teaching is generally measured by time on the job, so seniority in the public eye can be equated to expertise, a point that is challenged in Tsui's work.

A clear implication of this view is that experience creates expertise, but we know (and Tsui explains) the process is much more complex and nuanced than that. Here the saying that contrasts '20 years' experience or a year of experience 20 times' can capture a common public perception. The challenge is that there are still no accurate means to define publicly what it is the teachers whom we call 'expert', who are effective in the classroom, know and do. Some countries have schemes to document teachers' expertise (such as the US National Board for Professional Teaching Standards), but these are voluntary and differ from schemes that license teachers in public sector education. In language teaching, this lack of definition of teaching expertise is reflected when the default designation of 'native-speaker' is used to define language teachers' content knowledge. The widespread use of this default in many teaching, as well as general public, discussions illustrates how an outside-in concept can shape how teachers themselves see, and do, their work.

Lortie's 'egg-crate profession' is the reverse. It offers a powerful, inside-out metaphor for teaching that captures a central dynamic: the tension between autonomy and isolation. As teachers, we generally work alone as the only teacher in the room, like an individual egg in the cell of the egg-crate. This social arrangement of our work suggests that creating opportunities for collegiality and professional exchange (through conferences, study groups, teachers' meetings focused on development, and the like) as many forms of continuing professional development do, is an antidote. The same isolation can also be a source of professional satisfaction, however. Once we close the classroom door, we become autonomous decision-makers about the moment-to-moment unfolding of the lesson. There are certainly curricula to be taught, materials to be used, book chapters to be covered, and tests to be given. But the fabric of specifics are up to us with our students, with the implication that the range and type of these choices and decisions, and what happens from them, can be a source of professional learning and satisfaction.

5.3 How Teaching Is a Balancing Act Between Instructional Goals and Relational Work (Satisficing)

Lortie's study of teachers' work details a basic balancing act between instruction and classroom relationships. This is an instance where his analysis could be seen as negative, when it is actually articulating a tension that we all experience as teachers. It is a tension that is caught in the saying about 'teaching the lesson versus teaching the student'. This dichotomy is, of course, a false one: What the students do (or don't do) makes the lesson. But the implication is that as teachers, we balance responsibility for content and for students as learners, and this balancing act is at the heart of the work we do. Lortie uses the term 'satisficing' (explained in 1.2.3) to describe this balancing act. The term, which was prevalent in organisational theory of the period, is a bit dated, but its fundamentals are solid. Satisficing involves making decisions and choices with the aim of reaching the best outcome or result possible in the circumstances. Applied to the classroom as a work place, the idea of satisficing implies a lot about what teachers do. First, it implies that teachers need to know the content and their students as well as to understand the socio-professional context of their jobs. Second, it implies that these decisions range from those that may lead towards more desired outcomes to those that may not. Nothing is guaranteed in this work of teaching, but we do the best we can. We make decisions and evaluate the outcomes they lead to. Reflection is a third, clear implication. Satisficing is not playing darts in a dark room, throwing and hitting or missing a target. It is a process of learning from what you are doing as a teacher, even as you recognise that past experience does not guarantee future outcomes.

6. Implications of Huberman's Study

We see implications for teacher development in five areas in Huberman's study:

6.1 The amount of self-reflection and professional dialogue with colleagues that teachers are able to do

6.2 How the themes identified could be used in such self-reflection or collegial activity

6.3 Whether all teachers follow the same career stages and trajectories as the ones described in the study

6.4 What factors could constitute pedagogical competence

6.5 What attitude towards ourselves and our professional colleagues is most helpful

6.1 The Amount of Self-Reflection and Professional Dialogue With Colleagues That Teachers Are Able to Do

Towards the end of *The Lives of Teachers* in Chapter 10, 'Synthesis and Conclusion', Huberman writes, "The reader will certainly have noticed the absence in this study of 'recommendations' or 'practical suggestions'" (p. 261). He feels that in an exploratory study, such as his team's, the principal objective is to order the terrain. However, he does note an observation that many of the informants in the study, even those with 40 years or more of professional life behind them, had never really thought in depth about their initial motivation, the phases of their career, their levels of pedagogical mastery, their relationship to their institution, and so on. Yet they were glad to do so for many hours in the study. This suggests that the amount of self-reflection and professional dialogue with colleagues they had experienced had, thus far, been pretty rudimentary or superficial, squeezed out perhaps by the sheer volume of work and other commitments.

This leads Huberman to make two suggestions. One is that it could be of value to inscribe in the life of an educational institution some common havens for professional reflection around the themes in his study. The second suggestion is that a 'life cycle orientation' could influence the way that a school administration 'manages' teachers. Since the book you are now reading is primarily for teachers rather than school administrators, we need to think about what teachers can do alone or in collegial groups, even without the help of school administrators.

6.2 How the Themes Identified Could Be Used in Such Self-Reflection or Collegial Activity

Let us then draw out explicitly some of the themes that could, by implication from the study, be used in self-reflection or in collegial activity among and between teachers.

Themes for consideration could include: the initial motivations for entering the field of teaching and the evolution of those motives over time; the numbers of years in the job so far and a division of that time into phases or stages; the themes emerging for you, the teacher, in your phase or stage of work at the moment. Any themes that do seem to occur could be compared to those mentioned by teachers in the study. It could be interesting to consider our colleagues, how long they have been in teaching, and the phases and themes that are uppermost in their minds currently. A major area for deliberation might well be the creative responses possible in your context to your own and your colleagues' current themes, whether these themes involve easy or uneasy emotions.

6.3 Whether All Teachers Follow the Same Career Stages and Trajectories as the Ones Described in the Study

It is, as Huberman clearly states, quite possible that individual teachers skip one or more of the phases or stages mentioned in the study. Or a teacher might, instead, experience extra ones. When faced with a change in teaching situation, be it a change in course book or syllabus or in the level or age of students to be taught, one might well feel that one has slipped back to the early themes of 'survival' and 'discovery' after having been quite comfortably 'stabilised' for some time before! It could be interesting too to consider the long-term implications offered by the study for end-of-career satisfaction and to place ourselves. Have we enjoyed phases of in-class experimentation, the 'pedagogical tinkering' Huberman writes about? Or have we been more of an 'activist', going beyond the classroom and beyond our own institution to work, for example, on curriculum reform? These were possible indicators for the presence or absence of long-term career satisfaction.

6.4 What Factors Could Constitute Pedagogical Competence

An interesting part of Huberman's body of work is his careful production of a list of 18 factors constituting pedagogical mastery. The list was drawn from three streams of research and weighted towards studies of pedagogical needs expressed by teachers themselves. In the study great care was taken to prevent the list being seen as either a test to be passed by the teachers or as a norm to be adhered to. For use as an unfinished, open-ended list by a teacher on their own or in friendship groups, however, it could have considerable value.

6.5 What Attitude Towards Ourselves and Our Professional Colleagues Is Most Helpful

The overall orientation of the study reported implies that we need to stand on the side of the teacher. We need to understand that we and others may be in a particular and personal stage of our professional life cycle, may be experiencing an easy or a difficult theme at the moment, and may well need support. We may need to reflect or discuss with colleagues or otherwise work to devise creative responses to the stage and themes we are experiencing at this time. In short, the greatest implication of the Huberman study, in our view, is that we need to feel empathy, to be understanding, of our colleagues and of ourselves. To move into teaching, to settle into teaching, to experiment in our teaching, to avoid over-routinisation, to deal with relational distance or burn out or end of career pressures to secede . . . all these take imagination, energy, and support. We hope this book will help the endeavour by allowing you to see where you are, where you have come from, and where you would like to head next.

7. Implications of Tsui's Study

Tsui's work suggests implications for teacher development in five areas:

7.1 How we understand our own histories as teachers

7.2 How we relate to and use teaching knowledge

7.3 How we relate to our teaching contexts

7.4 How we negotiate the relationship between theory and practice

7.5 How we sustain our professional learning

7.1 How We Understand Our Own Histories as Teachers

How do we conceive of our own histories as teachers? We suspect that most of us would delineate our histories in terms of where, what, and whom we have taught. Tsui's research invites us to consider our history in two ways: in terms of critical incidents that shaped it, and in terms of what it means to be a novice, experienced, or expert teacher. By identifying critical incidents that have helped us to reframe our practice, we can better understand what matters to us and how we make sense of our teaching worlds.

Tsui acknowledges that development is hardly a linear sequence, although all experienced and expert teachers go through the novice phase. You may become a novice anew when the *where, whom,* and/or *what* you teach changes. One characteristic of novices is that they have a hard time attending to what, who, and how all at once. This raises the question of how you can use your expertise in areas in which you are a novice—for example, being able to draw on knowledge of how to engage learners—even while teaching new content. In terms of teacher development, this suggests that when faced with a new situation, we should be able to consciously identify what we know how to do that can be used in the new situation.

7.2 How We Relate to and Use Teaching Knowledge

One characteristic of expertise is the ability to integrate what we know about teaching and learning in our classroom practice so that any given activity contributes to a variety of learning objectives. According to Tsui, the ability to do this is rooted in having an elaborate knowledge base. But an elaborate knowledge-base is not enough if we tend to compartmentalised knowledge and plan in ways that separate rather than integrate that knowledge. One of the authors (Kathleen) once observed a primary school foreign language teacher whose students had the rotating responsibility for taking roll call, in the target language, in each lesson. This teacher did not compartmentalise classroom routines and language use; she integrated them. An implication for teacher development is to be able to identify ways in which we compartmentalise and ways in which we integrate knowledge and then to discern whether our practice could be more integrated.

7.3 How We Relate to Our Teaching Contexts

The notion that all learning is situated is central to Tsui's analysis of the teachers she studied. What teachers know and know how to do cannot be understood separately from the context in which they teach. Tsui writes, "Teachers' knowledge, therefore, must be understood in terms of the way they respond to their contexts of work, which shape the contexts in which their knowledge is developed" (p. 64). Experienced and expert teachers are able to identify factors in the context that constrain what they can do in the classroom. The expert teacher also sees the possibilities the context affords for agency, creativity, and choice. These possibilities may be most evident in the classroom, in which the teacher has the most power. However, Tsui pluralised the word *contexts*. This is important because the classroom context is embedded in the school, which is embedded in the wider community. Marina, the expert teacher, was able to see beyond the classroom to the way the wider social and policy context of the community affected students, and she used that knowledge to better teach them in the classroom. As a leader, she also actively sought to shape her department.

One implication for teacher development is to be able to identify constraints that we have been able to transcend successfully in order to learn from and build on that experience and, conversely, to be able to explore constraints that we have not been able to transcend. Another implication is the importance of finding ways to use the resources of our context to transcend the constraints or to look for affordances within the constraints. The myriad ways that teachers adapt textbooks to meet the needs of their students is a good example of this kind of understanding. Another implication is to be able to look beyond the classroom to identify the constraints that affect learners and the resources available in the wider community.

7.4 How We Negotiate the Relationship Between Theory and Practice

Tsui describes this relationship as bi-directional. On the one hand, expert teachers seek to understand or explain their practice 'from within' and to improve or reframe it based on these understandings. Tsui calls this theorising practical knowledge. Marina's ongoing reflection on whether her well-disciplined classroom was also an enjoyable classroom led her to change the way she handled discipline. On the other hand, teachers also learn about theory, and use it as a lens for understanding the reasons for what works and doesn't in their practice, or as a tool to shape or change their practice. Tsui calls this "practicalising theoretical knowledge" (p. 257). The changes Marina made to the way she conducted group work based on what she learned in her PCEd class is an example of this.

Implications for teacher development involve deepening our capacity to reflect and give voice to how we understand our practice; being able to identify what motivates us to seek out new sources of theory; and how we use theory to critique, change, and improve our practice.

7.5 How We Sustain Our Professional Learning

In discussing each teacher's history, Tsui looked at the role that critical incidents can play in helping a teacher reframe her practice. However, critical incidents are not sought out by the teacher; they happen. These incidents gnaw at us long after they happen and call for us to examine and learn from them, much like the bit of dirt in the oyster's shell that eventually becomes a pearl. Teachers can also actively seek ways to develop and sustain their practice. Tsui discusses three ways teachers sustain ongoing development: experimentation, problematising, and seeking challenges. She describes the way Marina purposefully experimented with different ways of doing things, problematised what she took for granted in order to reframe her practice, and sought challenges that engaged her at the edge of her competence. This suggests that understanding what motivates us to experiment in our practice is fertile ground for teacher development. Likewise, being able to question aspects of our practice that we take for granted can open up new ways of understanding or doing things. The final implication is to consider whether we welcome or seek out challenges and how they have contributed to expanding our competence.

Tsui ends her analysis by talking about multiple and distributed knowledge. The sign of an expert teacher is not that she knows everything and doesn't need help, but that she knows what she doesn't know and is able to seek support, guidance, and knowledge from others. This suggests that we should be able to see gaps in our knowledge as opportunities to draw on our colleagues' expertise and develop collegial support (as discussed in Part 4).

8. Implications of the *Learning4Teaching* Project

Although it is a large-scale study, the *Learning4Teaching* Project research has implications for individual teachers as they participate in professional development. We refer to two particular implications here:

> 8.1 How we make sense of professional development is a personal process
> 8.2 Professional learning involves making sense of (and from) learning opportunities

8.1 How We Make Sense of Professional Development Is a Personal Process

The *Learning4Teaching* Project demonstrates the personal, contextual, and unpredictable ways in which teachers make sense of professional development. As discussed earlier, the general view of the process of professional development, usually found in educational policies and reforms, is a causal one: that what is 'taught' in professional development is what is—or should be—'learned' by teachers. The *Learning4Teaching* Project suggests there is an alternative to this input-output view of professional learning—namely, that as teachers, we take part in professional development opportunities, which we then make sense of through our experiences in our classroom and school contexts. This process is a personal one, shaped by who we are and what we believe in.

8.2 Professional Learning Involves Making Sense of (and From) Learning Opportunities

One implication of point 8.1 above is that what we may get from a professional development opportunity depends on us. We engage in an active process of making sense of the input, even if the process can sometimes feel passive, as when listening to a speaker or looking at a slide show. The ideas from professional development events that make sense and that stay with us are the ones that we work out. From this perspective, implementing professional development is about transforming the learning opportunity into something we can use in our work. This transformation is a process of digesting input and making it part of our own thinking.

D. Looking Ahead

In Part 2, we move from implications of the research to application in practice. We take up the themes and implications from Lortie, Huberman, Tsui, and the *Learning4Teaching* Project and link them to teacher development activities that are designed to guide you in considering where you have come from, where you are now, and where you may be headed as a teacher.

Notes

1 To consider these ideas further, see Freeman (2016), particularly Chapter 2, and also Larsen-Freeman & Freeman (2008).

2 For a fuller discussion of the development of conceptions of teacher knowledge in language teaching and general education, see Freeman (2016).

3 To read two other very interesting discussions of these tensions or dilemmas inherent in teaching, see Berlak & Berlak (1981) *The dilemmas of schooling,* which writes about them from a macro, sociological level, while Lampert's (1985) classic article "How do teachers manage to teach", describes a teacher's view of the dilemmas of teaching.

4 The more common term is 'egg carton'.

5 Because the national survey was retrospective, the period of professional development referred to varied. In Chile and Turkey, the survey data was collected in 2012–13 about a PD period between 2007 and 2010; in Qatar, the data was collected in 2015–16 about the 2011–2104 period. We argue that the specific time periods do not alter the overall findings.

6 The survey was designed so that teachers could respond to survey questions in the national language (e.g. Spanish), in English, or in a mixture of the two languages.

From Implications to Application

A. Introduction

We ended Part 1 with a discussion of the implications of the research on teacher development over time—how that research can help us understand and shape our development as teachers. In Part 2, we describe teacher development activities that draw on the research and those implications. Thus, each activity is linked to some aspect of the research in Part 1.

Links Between the Research/Implications and the Activities

Below, we have created tables that summarise key concepts from the research of Lortie, Huberman, Tsui, and the *Learning4Teaching* Project. For each concept, we have drawn implications for professional development over time. We have then listed the activities that relate most closely to the concept and/or the implications. So if certain concepts and implications are of particular interest to you, you can go directly to those activities. Part 3, From Application to Implementation, provides suggestions for different ways to use the activities in your context.

In Table 2.1, we list key concepts from Lortie's research and their implications. The activities numbered and named in the third column address the concept and/or the specific implications.

In Table 2.2, we list key concepts from Huberman's research and their implications. The activities numbered and named in the third column address the concept and/or the specific implications.

Table 2.1 Lortie—Summary of implications and related activities

Concepts	Implications	Activities
How you were taught can help you understand how you teach	• What you liked/disliked about the instructional and relational aspects of your experience as students and how these may have shaped your current views	6 Ghosts Behind the Blackboard 10 Language-Learning Autobiography
How your work as a teacher as viewed from the outside contrasts with how you live it	• How you get people to understand what your work is really about • How you break down the cells of the egg crate • How you use your autonomy to sustain you	33 Describing My Work 35 Writing an Op-Ed 7 Talking Shop 13 How Do I Grow a Teaching Skill? 41 Who Is My 'Go To Person'?
How teaching is a balancing act between instructional goals and relational work	• What you know about your students and how that affects your work • What you know about content and how you represent it for your students • How you use reflection in your work	24 A Course Book Page We Love/Hate 25 They Keep Getting Younger! 26 How Do I See My Students? 27 Dialogue Journals 15 Doing What Makes Sense

Table 2.2 Huberman—Summary of implications and related activities

Concepts	Implications	Activities
The amount of self-reflection and professional dialogue with colleagues that teachers are able to do	• How you can build in times and places for professional reflection on themes identified below . . . • How you make sense of a 'life cycle' orientation	8 Yearly Retrospective 3 What Are My Own Professional Life Cycle Stages?
How the themes identified could be used in such self-reflection or collegial activity	• Your initial motivations for entering teaching • How you divide your time as a teacher into stages and identifying themes of each • Which stages have been easy/difficult • How you compare your own stages/themes with colleagues	1 How Did I Become an English Teacher? 2 My Career Graph 3 What Are My Own Professional Life Cycle Stages? 18 Facing a Difficult Stage in My Professional Life Cycle 19 How Can I Respond Creatively to a Difficult Stage of My Professional Life Cycle? 14 Checking Bad Habits! 31 From Tactics to Beliefs: The Four-Column Analysis

(Continued)

Table 2.2 (Continued)

Concepts	Implications	Activities
Whether all teachers follow the same career stages and trajectories as the ones described in the study	• Whether you have skipped stages, 'repeated' stages, and why • What characterises your present stage and how you envision your end of career stage	2 My Career Graph 3 What Are My Own Professional Life Cycle Stages? 51 Moving On: Collecting or Throwing Away? 52 Moving On, Heading Out
What factors could constitute pedagogical competence	• How different factors from Huberman's list apply (or don't apply) to you • How you would modify the list	20 How Can I Check My Pedagogical Competence?
What attitude towards ourselves and our professional colleagues is most helpful	• How you cultivate imagination and energy in your professional life so that you can respond creatively to each stage or theme • How you cultivate empathy and support for other teachers • How you learn from other teachers	48 I Plan, You Teach. You Plan, I Teach. 39 How Do I Grow a Teacher Learning Technique? 7 Talking Shop 34 Half-Scripted Interviews 41 Who Is My 'Go To Person'?

In Table 2.3, we list key concepts from Tsui's research and their implications. The activities numbered and named in the third column address the concept and/or the specific implications.

Table 2.3 Tsui—Summary of implications and related activities

Concepts	Implications	Activities
How you understand your history as a teacher	• How you understand the critical incidents that show you what matters to you • How you draw on what you already know when you become a 'novice' again	9 Critical Incidents 40 What's in My Teaching Suitcase? 45 From Known to New
How you relate to and use your teaching knowledge	• How you identify ways that you compartmentalise and ways that you integrate knowledge in your practice • How you discern ways to have greater integration	16 Exploring Dichotomies in Teaching Knowledge 17 Teaching Knowledge as 'Either/Or' vs 'Both/And'
How you relate to your teaching context	• How you understand the constraints and resources of the classroom, institution, and community • How you know your students • How you use the resources and transcend the constraints	32 Constraints and Resources of My Teaching Context 29 Freirean Problem Posing 24 A Course Book Page We Love/Hate 27 Dialogue Journals 38 A 'Good' Teacher Is . . .

(Continued)

Table 2.3 (Continued)

Concepts	Implications	Activities
How you negotiate the relationship between theory and practice	• How you deepen your ability to reflect on and give voice to why you do what you do • How you identify what motivates you to seek out new theories • How you use theory to critique, change, and improve your practice	11 Transformative Times 21 Letter to a Mentor 22 There Is Nothing So Practical as a Good Theory 23 Teaching Log
How you sustain your development	• How you experiment • How you problematise what you take for granted • How you seek challenges at the edge of your competence • How you seek support, guidance, and knowledge from others	11 Transformative Times 50 Breaking Rules 4 Material Changes 5 Methodological Changes 28 Building Case Studies 29 Freirean Problem Posing 30 Teaching Bump 44 Mapping the Future 41 Who Is My 'Go To Person'? 48 I Plan, You Teach. You Plan, I Teach.

In Table 2.4, we list key concepts from the *Learning4Teaching* Project and their implications. The activities numbered and named in the third column address the concept and/or the specific implications.

Table 2.4 *Learning4Teaching* Project—Summary of implications and related activities

Concepts	Implications	Activities
The connection between professional development and teaching is not causal	• How you view your participation in professional development: as receiving input or taking part in a learning opportunity	12 Professional Development Survey 23 Teaching Log 36 Two Maps of Professional Learning
Teacher learning is a process of making sense of (and from) learning opportunities	• What you may get from a professional development opportunity depends on you • How you make sense of the input as an active process (even if it can feel passive) • How the ideas that come to make sense and stay with you are the ones that you figure out and work with	15 Doing What Makes Sense 12 Professional Development Survey 23 Teaching Log

The above concepts provide a rich and multi-faceted way of approaching teacher development. Our interpretations of what the three 'trajectorist' researchers offer us share certain themes, but from different perspectives. For example, each addresses **history**—Lortie from the point of view of the apprenticeship of observation; Huberman from the point of view of self-identified stages; and Tsui in broader terms of novice, experienced, and expert as well as in specific terms of critical incidents that shape our experience. Each addresses **collegiality** (or its lack) in some way—Lortie with the metaphor of the egg-crate profession, Huberman with the need for collegiality, Tsui with the notion of distributed expertise. Each author considers **reflection** a core part of a teacher's practice and development. The *Learning4Teaching* Project suggests that a central feature of professional development is how teachers are able to make sense of the input from professional development events and transform what they learn into their practice. Collegiality was also a theme that emerged in this research—various teachers across the different national contexts noted that interacting with colleagues was an important part of their learning in the professional development events they participated in.

Organisation of the Activities in Part 2

The way we would like to bring together the concepts and implications in a practical way is to ask you to consider them from the perspectives of where you have come from as a teacher—your history; where you are now—your present concerns; and where you are headed—your hopes and intentions for the future. We have thus divided the activities into three sections, each with a guiding question. The guiding question for section B is *Where have I come from?* The activities in this section are designed to help you consider your past experience as a teacher and what you can learn from it. The guiding question for section C is *Where am I now?* The activities in this section are designed to help you consider where you are now in your career from a variety of perspectives and to help you understand what matters to you at this point in your development. The guiding question for section D is *Where am I headed?* The activities in this section are designed to help you look toward the future and what you want to do or be, going forward. In each of the sections, we have created a set of questions that will act as a framework for the practical activities.

From our perspective, the advantage of this way of organising the activities is that all except a very few can be used by any teacher, at any point in her or his career. We have not made a distinction between novice and experienced teachers. There are a few activities that probably work best for those who have some years of teaching experience (e.g. Activity 5, *Methodological changes*) but the majority can be fruitful for any teacher at any stage in her or his career. So, for example, an activity that asks you to chart your career thus far can be as fruitful for a teacher with one year of experience as for a teacher with 10 years of experience.

This approach means that all teachers, regardless of how long they have been teaching, can try out any of the activities from the perspective of where they are at this moment in their careers and professional development.

B. Where Have I Come From as a Teacher?

The activities in Section B encourage you to look back on your teaching life so far and consider what has happened and how the journey has been.

Activity 1: *How Did I Become an English Teacher?*
Activity 2: *My Career Graph*
Activity 3: *What Are My Own Professional Life Cycle Stages?*
Activity 4: *Material Changes*
Activity 5: *Methodological Changes*
Activity 6: *Ghosts Behind the Blackboard*
Activity 7: *Talking Shop*
Activity 8: *Yearly Retrospective*
Activity 9: *Critical Incidents*
Activity 10: *Language-Learning Autobiography*
Activity 11: *Transformative Times*
Activity 12: *Professional Development Survey*

From Implications to Application

The following are questions to consider:

- What is my teaching biography? What is my language-learning biography? What is my educational biography? How do these histories interrelate?

- How did I get into language teaching? What were my original motives?

- How does my background shape my assumptions as a teacher?

  - What kinds of schools and classrooms was I in as a student?

  - What teachers do I remember and why?

- What have been the most transformative experiences of language learning and in teaching to date?

Activity 1: How Did I Become an English Teacher?

Connections to research: Huberman suggests it can be useful for teachers to look back to consider their initial motivations for entering the profession and to see whether these have changed at all over time.

Materials

The list of questions below

A recording device (if you wish to do the alternative in Step 2 of Procedure)

Procedure

1. Consider the following questions and add any others on the topic that you would like:

   1. *How did you hear about the job of English teacher?*

   2. *Did you know anyone who was one?*

3. *What made you apply for your initial teacher training or your initial teaching job?*

4. *In what ways did you feel you would be able to do the job?*

5. *What did you hope for in becoming a teacher, for yourself, for your family and friends, for your future students, for your colleagues, your organisation, your country?*

6. *So, what's the story really of your becoming a teacher?*

7. *Once you'd got into the classroom and started teaching, did any of these hopes change?*

8. *How do you feel now? Do you think any of your initial hopes were unrealistic? What threads have stayed strong?*

9. *Do you have new or different hopes now? What's the biggest change?*

2. If working on your own, you can read the questions and consider your answers to them. But if you prefer, you can record yourself asking the questions. Then, play your recording back, pausing after each question to answer by inner monologue or out loud.

3. Alternatively, you can draw a picture to represent an answer to the question above that you feel is the most important.

4. If working with a colleague, go over the questions together, adding any others on the topic that you feel would be interesting. Decide if you will take one question at a time and answer it in turns or if you will let one person answer all the questions before giving the other person their turn.

5. Whether you do the activity alone or with a colleague or colleagues, take time to consider whether you have changed your motivation much since you started teaching and, if so, whether that matters to you or not.

Activity 2: My Career Graph

Connections to research: Huberman asked the teachers in his study to look back over their careers to date and to divide them up into phases or stages. He also asked the teachers to come up with names or themes for the phases they had identified. The activity below encourages you to map the phases of your career in the same way. It is worth considering too what you have learned as a teacher over time in all the phases.

Materials

Large sheets of paper (A3 or 11 1/2 × 14)

Coloured pens

Procedure

1. Think back over your professional life. Remember when you started teaching, when you may have moved institutions or teaching contexts, changed jobs or positions. Think back to major professional events (like advanced training, conferences, etc.) and consider where you are teaching now.

2. On a large sheet of paper, draw a line to represent your career path to this point. You may wish to include some gradual climbs, high points, low points, plateaux, and muddled sections.

3. Label these with approximate dates and make a few notes on the reasons for the highs and lows.

4. Decide how to subdivide the timeline for yourself, perhaps by years, teaching contexts, focal concerns, growth of expertise, or a mixture of these.

5. What do you notice? What do you find interesting or surprising about your graph? How would you describe the stages in your career to date?

6. This can be an individual reflection or, if you have a colleague to do this activity with, once you have made your graphs, you can share them, noting similarities and differences.

Extensions and Variations

Think about your current work situation and, looking ahead, extend the line for the next few years. Note any major events or changes in your work situation that you anticipate or would like. How would you project the next stage of your professional trajectory? Would you represent it as an upward, downward, or level trajectory going forward?

Activity 3: What Are My Own Professional Life Cycle Stages?

Connections to research: While describing phases that teachers in his study *can* go through, Huberman was very careful not to prescribe these as stages that other teachers *ought to* go through. It is useful therefore for teachers to consider the particular paths they have followed or are following in their careers.

Materials

Part 1 of this book

Procedure

1. Look back at Table 1.2 on page 19 of Part 1 of this book, together with the description of the stages in it.

2. Consider your own professional career to date. Then consider the following questions:

> Do you recognise any of the stages described and labelled by the teachers in Huberman's study?

> Have you skipped any of the stages they came up with?

From Implications to Application

> *Have you experienced similar stages but in a different order?*
>
> *Have you experienced the same sequence of stages over and over again?*
>
> *Have you inhabited more than one stage at the same time?*
>
> *Have you gone through or are you currently going through other stages not mentioned in the study?*

3. Finally, you might like to consider whether having similarities with teachers in the study is reassuring—and whether you can come up with reasons for any differences between yourself and teachers in the study.

Extensions and Variations

You can use the chart you created for Activity 2, *My Career Graph*, and refer to the chart to help you answer the questions in Step 2 of the Activity 3 Procedure.

Activity 4: Material Changes

Connections to research: Tsui suggests that when a teacher is able to reframe her understanding of something she takes for granted, to 'problematise' it, she is able to see it in a new light. By looking at materials we have used in a historical light, we may be able to understand them and how they shape or contribute to our practice in new ways.

Materials

The list of language learning materials provided below.

Procedure

1. Look at this list of language learning materials.

Banda machine	Felt board	Puppets
Realia	Blackboard	Cuisenaire rods
Audio active language lab	Tape recorder	Cassette recorder
CD player	Mp3	Course book
Graded readers	Teacher activity recipe books	Silent Way pointer
Magazine pictures	Musical instruments	Interactive Dialogue journals
Picture compositions	Video clips	Real photos
Board games and dice	Flashcards	Posters
White board	Interactive white board (IWB) or Smart board	Data projector
iPad or tablet	Radio	Headphones
Ear buds	Web 1.0 for information	Web 2.0 for interaction
Smart phone		

2.   Review the list, marking items as follows:

√ Put a tick or check by the ones you used regularly when you started teaching (e.g. blackboard, poster, Cuisenaire rods).

* Star the ones you use regularly now (e.g. course book, IWB, web 1.0 for information)

? Put a question mark by the ones you have never seen (e.g. banda machine, felt board, data projector)

! Use an exclamation mark for the ones you know others use but you haven't tried yet (e.g. smart phone, tablet, web 2.0 for interaction)

+ Add to the list any others that you know of or use.

3.   Looking over these five categories, think about the changes—positive and negative—you have had to make in your teaching as

a result of the changes in the materials you have used. What has remained the same? Are you achieving the same ends via different routes? Are there any aids you used to use that you miss? Are there any you would like to try?

Further Reading

Woodward, T. (2001). *Planning lessons and courses* (see especially chapter 5 'What can we teach with?') Cambridge: Cambridge University Press.

Activity 5: Methodological Changes

Connections to research: Tsui suggests that when a teacher is able to reframe her understanding of something she takes for granted, to 'problematise' it, she is able to see it in a new light. By looking at teaching methods we have used in a historical light, we may be able to understand them and how they shape or contribute to our practice in new ways.

Materials

None

Procedure

1. Look back at all the teaching methods you have come across and used in your teacher training and your practical teaching. Depending on how long you have been a teacher, these may include:

   Grammar Translation, The Direct Method, The Audio Lingual/ Visual Method, Silent Way, Suggestopedia, Community Language (or Counselling) Learning (CLL), Communicative Language Teaching, Task Based Learning, Total Physical Response, Dogme, Psychodramatic Language Learning, or others.

2.   Next, consider the various components of a method. Here are some example components:

   •   the materials usually associated with it

   •   the way the students and furniture are usually arranged

   •   the main aims of the method

   •   the beliefs that lie behind it

   •   the teacher and student roles

   •   the attitude toward error

   •   the order of the skills of reading, writing, speaking, and listening

   •   where the language to be learned comes from

   •   how the language is organised: Is it cut into bits? If so, of what size, and what is the order of the bits to be learned? Is it presented as whole texts?

   •   the topics that are often used

3.   Take a couple of methods that you have used in your teaching and consider the differences between them in the way they deal with the various components above. For example, in Grammar Translation, the skill order tends to be reading and writing first whereas in Communicative Language Learning, it tends to be listening and speaking first. In a class using Grammar Translation, the students tend to be seated in rows behind fixed desks, with the teacher sitting at the front of the class. In Communicative Language Teaching, the students are often in pairs or groups with movable desks and the teacher moves around the class a lot more. Working through the components of methods, see how they are dealt with in the methods you have chosen to compare.

4.   If you have lived through a change from, say, Grammar Translation to, say, Communicative Language Teaching, you will have had to, or have chosen to, change many components of your teaching. It can be

interesting to consider this and whether you have kept features of past methods you have used and continued to use them in your current work so that your teaching method has 'archaeological' layers to it!

5. As you work through the components and compare more of the methods you have used in your work, new ideas for components may occur to you, such as which of the five or six senses (touch, sight, etc.) is focused on most in a particular method or how testing and evaluation are dealt with from method to method.

6. Consider whether you actually agree with all the components of the method you are currently using. Think about whether what you are doing in class these days actually *is* a consistent, congruent method or instead an eclectic mix or integration of different elements with real reasoning behind it.

Extensions and Variations

For an amusing account of how a hapless student might suffer at the hands of different methodologists, see Church (1997).

Further Reading

Church, M. (1997). The parable of the good language learner. *The Teacher Trainer*, *11*(3), 9.
Woodward, T. (1997). Working with teachers interested in different methods. *The Teacher Trainer*, *11*(3), 7–9.

Activity 6: Ghosts Behind the Blackboard

Connections to research: Lortie introduced the phrase 'the apprenticeship of observation'. We spend many hours as children and young adults watching our own teachers at work. From this we absorb ideas about how to be a teacher and how not to be a teacher. We might make decisions about what we will always try to do in our classrooms or what we will never do. But can we stick to these decisions?

Materials

None

Procedure

1. Count up the total number of teachers you have had in your life in primary, secondary, tertiary, and further/adult education.

2. Remember a teacher/learning experience you thought was great and one that you felt was not so great. Remember as much as possible about these good and bad experiences. Where were you? How old were you? Who was the teacher? What happened? How did you feel? In this way, can you identify a good teacher from the past? And an unfortunate one? These are your good and bad teacher 'ghosts'.

3. If you have someone to work with, discuss these experiences with them and consider the effect these ghosts have had on your own work.

4. From then on, every time you have a bit of a puzzle after a lesson or an observation, you can ask yourself, 'What would my good ghost Ms X have done in this sort of situation?' Or use the idea to comment 'That's something my bad ghost Ms Z would have said!'

Further Reading

Weintraub, E. (1989). Interview. *The Teacher Trainer*, 3(1), 7–8.

Activity 7: Talking Shop

Connections to research: Lortie's metaphor of teachers being isolated in their individual cells in the 'egg-crate' suggests how cut off we can feel from fellow teachers. This activity brings teachers together to create bonds by talking about their experiences in a light-hearted but heartfelt way.

From Implications to Application

Materials

None

This activity works especially well when a group of teachers (20 maximum) with a few years' experience, and from different schools, decide on a topic (see examples below). They prepare an anecdote related to the topic and bring it to the meeting.

Procedure

1. Invite teachers to a 'Talking Shop' informal get-together of an hour or so outside work hours.

2. Set a topic such as 'My funniest teaching moment' or 'My most embarrassing teaching moment'. Ask participants to prepare a true anecdote from their experience on the topic and to bring it with them in note form. They should be prepared to tell that anecdote to the group.

3. If possible, allow for some food, drink, and music to greet people on the 'Talking Shop' night.

4. When everyone is seated in a circle after initial chitchat, explain the idea. Volunteers tell an anecdote. While a teacher is telling an anecdote, all listen attentively. Clarification questions are allowed, but there should be no praise or blame or interruptions. Hoots of laughter are okay unless the tale is a sad one. Expressions of sympathy are also fine.

5. If necessary, prime the pump with an anecdote of your own.

6. Don't go round the circle in order. Don't make anybody speak if they don't have an anecdote. Don't complain if the anecdote is a bit off the topic. Just allow for clarification questions and silence in between anecdotes. Usually anecdotes will trigger memories and then more anecdotes, so the pause won't last long.

7. When you have all had a chance to offer an anecdote, ask if people want to meet again for another 'Talking Shop' and, if they do, choose a new topic together.

Further Reading

Clark, C. (2001). *Talking shop: Authentic conversation and teacher learning*. New York: Teachers College Press.

Activity 8: Yearly Retrospective

Connections to research: As Huberman noted, professionally useful learning doesn't happen only at conferences or on courses. It can happen when we read, when we have conversations at or after a professional development (PD) session, when we do all manner of things such as watch a TV programme on stress busting, read new Health and Safety regulations, volunteer in an Oxfam book shop or homeless shelter, or do a new task within our job.

Materials

A file or plastic wallet or piece of paper or Word document.

Procedure

1. Think back over the past year and make brief notes on learning activities you have undertaken. Just note what prompted the learning, what the learning was, and how you feel it helps you in your job.

2. Write about 250 words, or more if you want, as a learning log. Flyers, articles, TV programme descriptions, tangibles, 'audibles', 'visibles', and other items can be collected if you'd like to make a professional learning scrapbook.

3. You can also think ahead to what you would like to do in terms of professional learning in the next year. The idea is not necessarily to spend any more time on your personal professional learning than you already do but to note down what you already do, briefly, perhaps throughout the year, spending an hour a year detailing or concretising the learning. This way you make it visible, in summary, to yourself and maybe to others too if you choose to share the log or to do this activity in a teaching team.

Activity 9: Critical Incidents

Connections to research: In Tsui's study, the expert teacher, Marina, was able to reflect on critical incidents involving students that were related to classroom discipline that she felt were 'regrettable'. In her reflection, she considered the incidents from the students' point of view. In doing so, she was able to shift her understanding of discipline as a matter of maintaining order to a matter of helping students learn. This activity asks you to identify such incidents in the past that have helped you to reframe your understanding of your practice.

Materials

None

Procedure

1. Think back over your history as a teacher and identify one or two incidents in your practice that you wish you had handled differently and that you feel had an impact on your practice in some way.

2. Choose one and write about it in the following sequence:

   - Describe and explain:

     When did it happen? Where did it happen? Who was involved? What was the sequence of events? Who said what? Who did what?

   - Provide rich, concrete facts:

     How did you feel during and after the incident? What emotions were evoked?

     Explain the event from the point of view of each participant:

     What precipitated the incident? Why did it happen? How did it feel?

- Analyse the general meaning and significance:

  What does the incident tell you about teaching and learning?

  Can you relate it to theories that are important to you?

- State your position:

  What does the incident tell you about what you believe as an educator?

- Describe the effects on your practice:

  What effect did the incident have on you and your practice?

  Did it change what you do? What you believe? How?

Further Reading

Griffin, M. L. (2003). Using critical incidents to promote and assess reflective thinking in preservice teachers. *Reflective Practice, 4*(2), 207–220.

Tripp, D. (2012). *Critical incidents in teaching: Developing professional judgment* (Routledge Education Classic ed.). London: Routledge.

Activity 10: Language-Learning Autobiography

Connections to research: Lortie's idea of the 'apprenticeship of observation', the ways we are socialised into teaching, can cover a range of experiences. For language teachers, our experiences as learners—both inside and outside of the classroom— contribute to strong ideas about what language teaching is 'supposed to be'.

Materials

A piece of paper on which to draw a time line

Procedure

1. Choose a language you studied in school. Make a time line that starts with your first contact with the language and goes until now.

2. On the time line, note significant experiences, both good and bad, that contributed to and affected your experience as a language learner. Put the good experiences above the line, with dates, and the bad experiences below the line, with dates.

3. Write an autobiography of yourself as a language learner. Use the significant experiences on the time line to shape your autobiography. In the autobiography, describe the kind of learner you are/ were, your motivation for learning the language, and your attitudes towards yourself as a speaker, reader, listener, writer of the language.

4. Read the autobiography and note links between your experiences and the way you teach: *What do you emphasise? What do you never do? What do you enjoy doing? Is there anything surprising or unexpected in these links?*

Activity 11: Transformative Times

Connections to research: Both Huberman and Tsui discuss the role of experimentation in teacher development. For many of Huberman's teachers, experimentation led to career satisfaction. A critical difference between Tsui's expert teacher and the other teachers was her engagement in ongoing experimentation, often at the edge of her competence.

Materials

None

Procedure

1. Look back over your teaching experience and try to remember times when you really changed something—perhaps your approach to students or your materials or methods. Reading the example below may help to trigger your memories.

Example of a transformative experience

The setting

Saturday morning classes in Japan, 9 am to 12 noon. Six adult students who had worked all week in their normal jobs. The class was called 'English Conversation'. The students got on fine with each other and with the teacher. On paper, their level was intermediate. They needed to speak more English in their jobs. There were plenty of resources available and the room was pleasant.

The puzzle

The students were so afraid of making mistakes and so shy in English that, no matter what I tried, I could not get more than about two words out of any student. They looked. They listened. They smiled. They did not speak much at all.

Asking for help

After trying every type of material and prompt I could think of over several weeks, I went to my Director of Studies (DOS) to talk it over. He listened carefully and then gave me an article to read. It was from a practical teaching magazine and was all about Community Language Learning (CLL).

The clue

I read the article. It described a process where students sit in a circle facing each other. The teacher sits outside the circle and has no eye contact with the students. There is a recording device on a table in the middle of the student circle. Once the students are told how to proceed, the teacher does not start or initiate anything. The students decide what they will talk about in the session. A student then tries to formulate whatever they want to say, in English. They turn to the teacher, who is outside the circle, so behind them, to check that their utterance is correct. If necessary, the teacher can whisper corrections into the student's ear and the student can practice the utterance as many times as they like before turning to the others, picking up the recording device and, speaking into it, saying what they wish to say to the others. The recorder is switched off again and goes back on the central table until another student wishes to say something to the group.

There was a lot more to the process but that is the basics of how the process starts.

My action

Well, I was so desperate that, though the idea seemed pretty weird, I decided to try it. The article had prepared me for the fact that I must be patient, especially at the beginning, and avoid leading, interrupting, and even making eye contact with students while they first faced each other in the circle and had to initiate something. I toughed it out and the first time we tried it, it sort of worked. I kept it up and after a few weeks it was really working. The students were deciding their own topics and speaking and I could transcribe the recordings for them to read later, thus proving to them that they had spoken—and spoken correctly in English, too.

The learning

I learned so much from this experience . . .

I learned that I could ask for help with my teaching, that there were magazines full of ideas for teachers, that I didn't have to be central in the classroom, that silence in the teacher was okay, that I could try different ideas out, that some might work, that I could be a kind of experimenter in my own classroom.

The follow up

When I went back to the article to re-read it for more detail on the process, I found a reading reference at the bottom. I followed it up and learned a lot more about CLL and the philosophy of its founder, Charles Curran. The learning has made a huge difference to my understanding of and behaviour in groups of all kinds.

2.   Once you have located a time in your own teaching experience when something in your knowledge, attitudes, skills, methods, or

materials changed, write it up under sub headings such as the ones in the account above.

3. Offer to share your account with colleagues as a basis for discussion of your own and their transformative times, or send it to a local, national, or international teaching newsletter or web site and see if you can get it printed or posted.

Further Reading

Larsen-Freeman, D., & Anderson, M. (2011). *Techniques and principles in language teaching*. New York: Oxford University Press.
Stevick, E. (1980). *Teaching languages: A way and ways*. Boston: Heinle Cengage.

Activity 12: Professional Development Survey

Connections to research: Teachers in Chile, Turkey, and Qatar completed a survey as part of the *Learning4Teaching* Project. This activity asks you to answer three of the most important questions that were on the survey. These questions are completely open-ended, which means you can answer them in any way you like. You will then have an opportunity to revisit your answers to the questions in Activity 23, *Teaching Log*.

Materials

A chart similar to this one:

	Name of PD event	Brief description	What did you learn?	If you were able to use it in your practice, how did you use it?
#1				
#2				
etc.				

From Implications to Application

Procedure

1. Think back over the last three years. List up to five professional development events you participated in during that time. (If you have been teaching less than three years, consider the time since you started teaching and list up to five professional development events you have participated in.) In the *Learning4Teaching* survey, a professional development event was defined as:

    > *A short or longer term activity (like a workshop or course) that may be delivered by a trainer on a new topic or issue either within or outside the school to support your teaching of English.*

2. For each event, complete the chart as follows:

    > Give it a **name** and then briefly **describe** it.

    > Describe **what you learned** from the event.

    > *If* you were able to use what you learned, explain **how you used it** in your practice.

3. Review each event: how you described it, what you learned from it, and how you used it.

    > How did you make sense of the event?

    > Did you learn or use what you learned as the providers of the event intended? How?

    > Or did you adapt what you learned to your particular context? How?

    Or did you learn something different from what the providers might have intended? Why?

    For example, in the surveys the teachers completed in Chile, one teacher filled in the last three columns of the chart as follows:

Brief description	What did you learn?	How did you use it in your practice?
Attendance at a course for the improvement of English	to help students develop the skills	for oral communication

What's interesting is that the aim of the course was described as helping *teachers* improve their English skills, but the learning and use were about helping *students* improve their skills. So the teacher who described events in this way found ways to use how they improved their own skills to help their students improve theirs.

In the surveys the teachers completed in Turkey, one teacher filled in the chart this way:

Brief description	What did you learn?	How did you use it in your practice?
Developing 4 skills in language teaching: Reading, writing, listening, speaking	I had opportunities to share experiences with teachers in other European countries	I adapted the different activity types I learned to the topic of the lesson

For this teacher, the importance of learning from and with other teachers regardless of the content is clearly important. The ideas for adapting the activities might come from talking to different teachers about how they would use what they learned about in the PD event.

4. Consider all of the events together. Do you notice any similarities between them? Any differences? Does anything surprise you?

From Implications to Application

5. If you are working with a colleague or colleagues, exchange what you have written. What kinds of similarities and differences do you see in the types of events you describe, what you learned from them, and how you used them?

———————

In Section B you have considered how you got started in your career as a teacher and how you got where you are. You've had the opportunity to explore, among others, the interrelationship of your experiences as a learner and as a teacher, your original motives for becoming a teacher, stages in your career thus far, changes you have witnessed over time, and transformative experiences of language learning and teaching that have influenced you. In the next section, we turn from the past to the present.

C. Where Am I Now?

Having considered the start of your teaching career and how you got to where you are, the activities in Section C encourage you to think about what you are doing in the present in your work. They encourage you to consider what you now know how to do and what you still do not know.

Activity 13: *How Do I Grow a Teaching Skill?*
Activity 14: *Checking Bad Habits!*
Activity 15: *Doing What Makes Sense*
Activity 16: *Exploring Dichotomies in Teaching Knowledge*
Activity 17: *Teaching Knowledge as 'Either/Or' vs 'Both/And'*
Activity 18: *Facing a Difficult Stage in My Professional Life Cycle*
Activity 19: *How Can I Respond Creatively to a Difficult Stage of My Professional Life Cycle?*
Activity 20: *How Can I Check My Pedagogical Competence?*
Activity 21: *Letter to a Mentor*
Activity 22: *There Is Nothing So Practical as a Good Theory*
Activity 23: *Teaching Log*
Activity 24: *A Course Book Page We Love/Hate*
Activity 25: *They Keep Getting Younger!*

Activity 26: *How Do I See My Students?*
Activity 27: *Dialogue Journals*
Activity 28: *Building Case Studies*
Activity 29: *Freirean Problem Posing*
Activity 30: *Teaching Bump*
Activity 31: *From Tactics to Beliefs: The Four-Column Analysis*
Activity 32: *Constraints and Resources of My Teaching Context*
Activity 33: *Describing My Work*
Activity 34: *Half-Scripted Interviews*
Activity 35: *Writing an Op-Ed*
Activity 36: *Two Maps of Professional Learning*

The following are questions to consider:

- What stage of my professional life am I in? What issues in teaching matter to me now?

- What stages are my colleagues in? What issues are they focused on?

- What are the key teaching issues I am working on now?

  - What am I good at in my teaching? What bothers me?

  - What changes and challenges to who I am as a person and a teacher do I see at this stage?

  - How has theory informed these issues?

- What is new or changing in my teaching situation? How is it influencing me, what I do, and what I'd like to do?

- How does my context influence my decisions? What impact do I have on my context?

- What can I learn from others (fellow teachers, supervisors) at this stage?

- What can I learn from my students at this stage?

- How can I stay motivated and realistically expand my professional horizons and work towards career goals?

Activity 13: How Do I Grow a Teaching Skill?

> **Connections to research**: Huberman suggests that, after moving through the initial stages of our work as teachers, we start to establish some useful routines. This activity encourages us to look at how this skill building continues over time and even into our more experienced years.

Materials

None

Procedure

1. Look back to a classroom skill that was emphasised when you were being trained, such as, for instance, asking clear questions to check students' understanding of what you're teaching.

2. Consider how much you have learned since then about performing this skill (e.g. how to plan your questions, make them clear, unambiguous and precise, use a range of question types such as open and closed, learning NOT to simply ask 'Got it?' or 'Everybody understand?' and knowing why this latter type of question is not advisable).

3. Next, use a range of reading materials (see example reference below) to understand how much more there is still to learn about the skill you have chosen. In this instance, for example, allowing 'wait time', at two different junctures, and 'wait time' of increasing length, while tracking the class and keeping attention focused and also understanding the reasons why this is advisable.

4. Consider how you will work on the new aspects of the skill you have chosen. It may well be that you will want to script new classroom interventions, plan new moves, discuss these with a colleague, try them out with peers, practice them quite a bit, and maybe record

yourself or ask for a peer to observe before taking them into your normal classroom. You will need to feel confident about the change you are making before risking it for real.

5. Once you have taken the change into your practice and tried it for a while, you will need to judge whether it is justified by an increase in student learning. You will also want to refine it further for there is always more to learn!

Extensions and Variations

Follow up by listing other things that you remember as being emphasised when you were in your initial training. Examples here could be: planning lessons; using your voice, posture, and movement; organising the room, furniture, and students; using a text book; making visual aids; correcting errors. Taking one skill at a time, consider what you have learned about that skill so far. Then figure out how you can search out what there still is to learn. Figure out ways you can practice and test out these new extensions of known skills and then how you can introduce them gradually into your classroom teaching.

From Known to New (Activity 45) uses ideas from this activity as the basis for considering the knowledge and skills we bring to a new situation. In new situations, we may feel like novices but in fact bring a great deal of experience to draw on.

Further Reading

Lemov, D. (2015). *Teach like a champion 2.0*. San Francisco, CA:-Bass.

Activity 14: Checking Bad Habits!

Connections to research: Huberman suggests that, after moving through the initial stages of our work as teachers, we start to establish some useful routines. This activity encourages us to look at the fact that we may also have gathered some non-useful routines!

From Implications to Application

Materials

None

Procedure

1. The first step is to think of ways to find out our bad habits. As it can be extremely difficult to recognise our own bad habits and hard to get other people to tell us what they are, we will need to be creative about finding out about our foibles. We will need to get information somehow. Here are some possible sources:

   - student end of week/term feedback forms

   - self-recording and watching/listening back

   - post peer observation discussion

   - results of asking students the question, 'What is the one thing you wish I would stop doing?' in their dialogue journals (see Activity 27).

   You could also try watching others at work, others you admire for their expertise or gift in some aspect of teaching. Check out Lemov (2015) or trawl YouTube for views of excellent teachers.

2. Next, identify what you *do*. Bear in mind that bad habits can include things that we do such as: echoing, giving rambling instructions, cramming the board with scribbly hand writing, asking 'Does everyone understand?', wasting time by passing out all the handouts ourselves, asking 'cat and mouse questions' where we end up pouncing on students who come up with answers different to the one we want.

3. Identify what you *don't* do. Don't forget to look out for errors of avoidance, things that we don't do. Examples here are skipping work on pronunciation, never getting to the 'free practice' part of a lesson plan, forgetting to attribute copyright on handouts taken from published sources, not allowing wait time after our own questions or again after student answers.

4. Once you have an idea of some bad habits you have got into, start
    with one you would like to change. Have a think about why it's
    a bad habit, why it's not helpful, but also why you do it or why it
    became a habit. For example, maybe you have got into the habit
    of raising your voice to get order in class. Maybe this is common in
    your school. However, this habit may be unhelpful for you as shout-
    ing can ruin your vocal cords. Maybe you hate silence and so often
    answer your own questions. This is unhelpful because your students
    will learn that they don't have to be active. Rushing off a minute
    before the final bell is not very helpful for any colleagues who are
    taking your class next morning. Thinking through the effects of our
    habits on other people will increase our motivation to change our
    bad habits.

5. Generally speaking, it is pretty difficult simply to give something up
    without replacing it with something else. That's why people trying to
    quit smoking tend to try drinking a glass of water, applying a nicotine
    patch, sniffing a jar full of old cigarette butts, or chewing gum when
    they have the urge to smoke a cigarette. So try to come up with
    something that will help you to amend your wicked way. For exam-
    ple, if you know you never wait long enough after asking your stu-
    dents a question, ask the question and then count 'One Mississippi,
    Two Mississippi', to yourself. Or count from one to ten internally,
    or say to yourself, 'I am going to calmly and pleasantly look round
    the room to include all the students in my gaze', or spend the time
    checking that your next utterance will be well phrased.

6. Involve your colleagues by telling them what you think your bad
    habit or error of avoidance is, why you want to change it, and what
    ideas you have come up with so far to help yourself. They may well
    come up with amusing or creative support ideas. It might also give
    the needed incentive to actually change the bad habit.

Further Reading

Lemov, D. (2015). *Teach like a champion 2.0*. San Francisco, CA: Jossey-Bass.

Activity 15: Doing What Makes Sense

Connections to research: There are several ways to look at how your sense-making as a teacher—what you do and why you do it—changes over time. You can consider how your sense-making is reflected (or not) in the broad stages in Huberman's study. You can also think about Lortie's idea of 'satisficing'—balancing personal relations with students and the needs and goals of your lessons—and how that dynamic in your teaching changes over time.

Materials

A grid like this one:

A teaching activity I . . .	
did when I was starting out . . .	and continue to do . . .
did when I was starting out . . .	but don't do anymore . . .
didn't do when I was starting out . . .	but do now . . .

Procedure

1. Prepare a grid (see sample above).

2. Think about activities in your teaching now compared to how you taught when you first started out. Fill in the gird with your answers to these questions.

   - *What is something that you used to do as a teacher and you still do?*

   - *What is something you used to do as a teacher, and you no longer do now?*

   - *What is something you do now that you didn't do when you started as a teacher?*

3. Consider the following questions:

   Why have some of these activities survived in your teaching while others haven't? What influenced you to stop or start doing a particular activity?

   What do you notice about changes in your teaching over time? How has your sense-making changed?

4 To pull your ideas together, you can discuss with others or make notes for yourself.

Activity 16: Exploring Dichotomies in Teaching Knowledge

Connections to research: Tsui describes how the teachers in her study would often separate facets of knowledge in their teaching. They would *compartmentalise* specific aspects of what they did so, for example, one teacher was happy that her students were able to express their values in writing even if they did not pay attention to the formal criteria for a well-written essay. This teacher separated 'student investment' (expressing values) from 'achieving learning objectives' (improving writing skills), seeing them as an 'either/or', which Tsui refers to as 'dichotomizing' teaching knowledge.

Materials

Large sheets of paper

Procedure

1. There are many dichotomies in language teaching: accuracy or fluency; communication or grammar; receptive skills or productive skills; games or serious work. Working either individually and then sharing your lists, or collectively, make a list of dichotomies that are present in your teaching.

2. Sort the list into three groups—the dichotomies that are about *the content* that you teach, about *your students* and their roles in the

classroom, and about you and *your role as a teacher*—like the chart below. We have put some examples in the chart from our own experience. You can make a fourth group as a 'parking lot' for those dichotomies that don't seem to fit readily into one of these three areas.

The content	Your students	Your role as a teacher
Meaning *or* form	Talkative *or* quiet	Encourager *or* challenger
Authentic *or* contrived	Believer *or* doubter	
Vocabulary *or* grammar	Those who prefer to work alone *or* with others	Correction-giver *or* understander
Speaking *or* writing		Up-front controller *or* facilitator
Emotionally positive topics *or* downers	Physically active *or* inactive	Talkative model-giver *or* quiet listener

3. Think about and discuss where each of these dichotomies seems to come from. Is it from your training as a teacher? From what is considered 'best practice' in ELT? From your institution? From social expectations of students (and parents)? From fellow teachers?

4. Now choose a specific class you taught recently. Make a detailed description of what you and your students did in the class.

5. Review the description of your class. Ask yourself, how did the dichotomies you listed show up in this lesson?

Note: This activity can be continued with Activity 17.

Activity 17: Teaching Knowledge as 'Either/Or' vs 'Both/And'

Connections to research: Tsui argues that expert teachers often go beyond thinking in terms of dichotomies and compartmentalizing knowledge to *integrate* aspects of their understanding of teaching and learning—in other words, to see them as 'both/and'. An example might be in thinking about classroom management; they would not see it as *either* classroom management *or* learning, but would see classroom management as an opportunity for learning.

Materials

Large sheets of paper

Procedure

1. Choose a specific class you taught recently, and make a detailed description of what you and your students did in the class. (You may want to re-use the description from Activity 16, Step 4). Here is a short example from a beginning-level Spanish class with students aged 12.

    > The teacher wrote five vocabulary words on the board that described people (e.g. tall, athletic).

    > She showed students pictures of people and called on students to describe them, using the vocabulary. For example, a student described a soccer player as tall and athletic.

    > The teacher then gave a brief introduction to the Mexican Day of the Dead in English. The teacher played a video in Spanish about the Day of the Dead while the students coloured in pictures of sugar skulls—elaborate skulls made of sugar for this holiday.

2. Review your description of your class from Step 1. Ask yourself, in what ways did I *compartmentalise* my knowledge about teaching and learning? For example, from the Spanish class above, the teacher:

    - Separated and thus compartmentalised 'vocabulary' and 'culture'.

    - Compartmentalised 'student activity' and 'content'—what students did while watching the video (colouring pictures) and the content of the video. She did not try to link the students to the content.

From Implications to Application

3. Review your description and ask yourself, in what ways do I *integrate* my knowledge about teaching and learning? Again, in the example from the Spanish class, the teacher could have:

- Used pictures and vocabulary to develop background knowledge about the video.

- Given students tasks to understand, talk about, and show what they learned from the video.

Extensions and Variations

Write your usual lesson plan for an upcoming class. Ask yourself the following questions about your plan:

- In what ways does this lesson compartmentalise learning?

- In what ways am I integrating what I know about content, students, and teaching?

- In what ways could there be more integration?

Activity 18: Facing a Difficult Stage in My Professional Life Cycle

Connections to research: Some teachers in Huberman's study described phases in their professional lives that were not, in their view, optimum. This implies that many of us English teachers may experience difficult times professionally, too. First, we need to recognise what times we are in.

Materials

Large piece of paper and coloured pens or, if you prefer, mind mapping software

Procedure

1. If you are feeling uncomfortable, ill at ease, or unhappy at work, give yourself time to consider your current professional situation. There are activities in this book to help you to do this—for example, *My Career Graph* (Activity 2), *What Are My Own Professional Life Cycle Stages?* (Activity 3), *An Eddy in the River* (Activity 46).

2. It may also help to make a mind map with the words '*Where I am with my job*' written in the centre of a large sheet of paper. This is your seed phrase. Draw branches out from the central seed and label them to represent what you feel are the main parameters of your professional life. Example branch labels might be 'Location', 'Colleagues', 'Students', 'School buildings', 'Syllabus', 'Pay and conditions', 'My competence' (See Activity 20, *How Can I Check My Pedagogical Competence?*) Next, make notes as to the positive (+) and negative (–) or interesting (!) points of each facet of your job.

3. By doing Steps 1 and 2 you have represented, in mind map form, how things are in your own current work reality. Take a minute to make sure you have left nothing out. Then look to see what connections there are among the various elements. Feel free to draw arrows between things that are connected, and to change font thickness for elements that now stand out. Add colour, too, depending on what you feel is going well (green or blue?) or badly (red?). Add sticky notes, draw thunderclouds, anything that expresses your situation. You may then decide to redraw your mind map as new understandings come to you while considering your first one.

4. Next, look at your mind map for a while, take it all in and then, after a couple of deep breaths, allow things to be as they already are. *How Can I Respond Creatively to a Difficult Stage of My Professional Life Cycle?* (Activity 19) will help you to react to things as they are. But, for now, simply look at your mind map as it is and allow things to be as they already are. If you discover that you are in fact deeply depressed

about your work situation, resolve to get some professional help. The following activity may also help for a start.

Extensions and Variations

Explaining your mind map to someone else can be a crucial step to help you clarify and understand what you are trying to portray.

Further Reading

If you are unfamiliar with mind maps, see the website below by the founder, Tony Buzan, and try his free, online, interactive course: www.tonybuzan.com/about/mind-mapping/

Buzan, T. (2009). *The mind map book: Unlock your creativity, boost your memory, change your life*. London: BBC Active.

Activity 19: How Can I Respond Creatively to a Difficult Stage of My Professional Life Cycle?

Connections to research: As mentioned in Activity 18, some teachers in Huberman's study described phases in their professional lives that were not, in their view, optimum. After we have recognised that we are in difficult times, how can we start to respond?

Materials

Optional: coloured paper

Procedure

Once you have realised that you are in a less than optimum phase of your professional life and have clarified its characteristics and facets, perhaps by trying out *Facing a Difficult Stage in My Professional Life Cycle* (Activity 18), you will want to react creatively to your current situation. Doing an activity that is somewhat analytical can help you to deal with the emotions you may be feeling. There are many thinking frameworks available, catalysts designed to get our thinking out of its ruts. One of these is Edward de Bono's 'Six Thinking Hats'.

1. You can make six paper, or metaphorical, hats of different colours. Each colour represents a different perspective or way of thinking about things. So we have:

    •   **White** for factual, unemotional, neutral exploration of what we know or need to know

    •   **Red** for the emotional, feelings, hunches, and intuitions

    •   **Yellow** is for a positive, optimistic view, of value and benefit

    •   **Black** is a judgmental, pessimistic point of view, the dangers and difficulties and why something may not work

    •   **Green** is for fresh, creative, alternative possibilities and new ideas

    •   **Blue** is 'meta' thinking, managing the thinking process, making sure the guidelines for all the other hats are followed. It gives an overview.

2. Metaphorically, put on the first five hats in turn and take time to consider your situation from that point of view. For example, when putting on the white hat, you may want to list facts, unaffected by your own opinions about them, or to write a brief description of what you know for certain and think about what you still need to know. When putting on the red hat, consider how you feel, what your gut instincts are, what one word or phrase sums up your emotions on the issue. Don't hold back. Allow yourself to have instincts and hunches. When putting on the black hat, go for the worst-case scenario. What are the worst aspects of the situation? And what is the worst thing that can happen? What are the dangers and difficulties? Be pessimistic! When putting on the yellow hat, look for the positive or potential 'silver linings' in your situation. What good things have come, could come, from the situation? What if all went well? Probe for value and benefit.

3. Once you have tried the first five colours, one by one, move to the last, blue, hat. Check you have followed the guidelines for all the

other hats. Consider if you need more information. Do you recognise your feelings more, notice more upsides or downsides than before? Any new ideas? What stood out for you as you tried on each hat? What avenues for action have now opened up? What dead-ends or ruts did you perceive? As you list your possible actions and reactions, you can take each one in turn and put on different hats when considering them too.

Extensions and Variations

If working with colleagues or friends on this, you can all wear the same hat, metaphorically, at the same time and brainstorm from that colour perspective. Alternatively, you can self-select, allocate or rotate different colour hats and discuss from a number of different perspectives at the same time.

Further Reading

De Bono, E. (1985). *Six thinking hats*. Boston: Little Brown.
Woodward, T. (2006). *Headstrong: A book of thinking frameworks for mental exercise.* (pp 60–64). Elmstone, UK: TW Publications.

If you are tempted to consider catalytic thinking frameworks as social science, as theory empirically proven to improve results, then read Bennett (2013) as an antidote:

Bennett, T. (2013). *Teacher proof: Why research in education doesn't always mean what it claims, and what we can do about it*. Abingdon, Oxon: Routledge.

Activity 20: How Can I Check My Pedagogical Competence?

Connections to research: When considering teacher competence, Huberman favoured a list of facets of pedagogical competence thought to be essential *by the teachers* in his study, rather than predetermined lists of facets that teachers had to be good at in order to become certified. Teachers in the study were encouraged to consider how they were doing in terms of each facet they had listed.

Materials

The list below

Procedure

1. Consider the list below, adapted from Huberman's study, of possible areas of pedagogical competence. Add any items that you feel are missing and strike out any you feel are irrelevant to you.

Areas of pedagogical competence

Good rapport with students

Keeping calm in difficult moments

Feeling at home with colleagues

Getting on with heads and principals

Dealing with discipline problems

Having good rapport with parents

Designing interesting lessons

Putting the right level of demand on students

Bringing the students back after you've 'lost' them

Covering the programme at an appropriate pace

Accepting feedback from colleagues

Dealing with heterogeneous classes

Motivating uninterested students

Assisting weaker students

Challenging stronger students

Feeling at the same level as experienced colleagues

From Implications to Application

Running small experiments

Working on your own personal and professional development

Continuing to gain content knowledge

2. In Huberman's study, teachers were invited to rate themselves as: 'Very competent', 'Competent', 'Adequate', or 'Under-developed' for each facet in the list. If you like these labels, then use them in the next step. If not, feel free to alter them or create your own labels.

3. Apply Huberman's labels, or the ones you have created, to each item in your list.

4. Look over how you have rated yourself. Does this give you any ideas of areas of work that you would like to improve in?

Further Reading

Huberman, M. with Grounauer, M., & Marti, J. (1993). *The lives of teachers*. London: Cassell. Chapter 9.

Activity 21: Letter to a Mentor

Connections to research: This activity draws on what Tsui calls "practicalising theory"—that an important source of teacher development is how we use theory to critique, change, and improve our practice.

Materials

None

Procedure

1. Make a list of people in language education whose ideas/theories have influenced you in some way.

2. From the list, choose one person whose ideas or popularisation of those ideas have had a *significant* impact on how you think about teaching and learning.

3. Name a key idea/theory (or ideas/theories, if more than one) that this person developed, exemplified, or popularised.

4. For each idea, make notes about:

    • how you understand its meaning

    • why it is important to you

    • two or three ways in which it is manifest in your practice

    • questions that have arisen about it for you

5. Write a letter to the person in which you describe the impact her, his, or their work has had on you. Use the notes you made in Step 4 to guide you.

Activity 22: There Is Nothing So Practical as a Good Theory

Connections to research: As in *Letter to a Mentor* (Activity 21), this activity draws on what Tsui calls 'practicalising theory' (i.e. using theory to change and improve your practice).

Materials

None

Procedure

1. Choose an idea, theory, framework. or article that has had a particular impact on your teaching. For example, for Marina, the expert teacher in Tsui's study, one important idea was that group work was not just a way to get people to use English with each

other. It should also have a purpose that could only be accomplished by a group and should have an outcome that could be shared with others.

2. Write a brief (1–2 sentence) explanation of the idea, framework, or article. (You will write more about it in the next step.)

3. Remember when you first encountered the idea. How did you understand it at the time? Why did it have an impact on you?

4. Then think of specific ways that it first influenced your teaching, ways that you tried to 'practicalise' it. What was challenging about it? What was rewarding?

5. How is the idea now manifest in your practice? Has your thinking about the idea changed? What would you add to, change, or question about the idea, framework, or article?

Activity 23: Teaching Log

Connections to research: In the *Learning4Teaching* project, teachers from Chile, Turkey, and Qatar completed a survey about their professional development during the previous 3 years. (That survey is the basis for *Professional Development Survey* (Activity 12).) Some of those teachers later kept teaching logs for up to 7 days. In the log, which they completed after they taught each day, they linked what they did before, during, and after teaching their lessons to the professional development activities they had described in the survey.

Materials

Teaching Log Template below (to be filled in/answered each day you keep the log):

Teaching Log

Focus and level of the class you are writing the log about:

_____

Professional development event that you are writing the log about:

_____

1. Did you use anything (ideas, techniques) from the professional development event in today's class?

2. If you *didn't*, why not?

3. If you *did*, which of the following areas were influenced by it?

   - Planning the lesson. Choosing or preparing the activities or materials I used in the lesson.
   - Presenting new material in the lesson.
   - Having students practice or use the new material in the lesson.
   - Monitoring and responding to what students did in the lesson.
   - Managing group work in the lesson.
   - Interacting with the students.
   - Assessing students' learning.
   - Reflecting on the lesson after it was done.
   - Connecting and interacting with other teachers.
   - Other?

4. If you *did*, describe a specific example from your class in which the professional development event was useful to your teaching.

Procedure

1. Identify a professional development event you have participated in during the last 2 or 3 years. (If you have been teaching less than 3 years, consider the time since you started teaching and list up to

five professional development events you have participated in.) In the *Learning4Teaching* survey, a professional development event was defined as:

> *A short or longer term activity (like a workshop or course) that may be delivered by a trainer on a new topic or issue either within or outside the school to support your teaching of English.*

> Note: if you have completed *Professional Development Survey* (Activity 12), then choose one of the PD events you wrote about for that activity.

2. Choose one class you teach to focus on. For example, if you teach three different levels of students, choose one. If you teach classes with different content (e.g. reading, English for engineers, academic writing), choose one.

3. For the next week of teaching, at the end of each day, fill out the log described in Materials, above.

4. At the end of the week, read through your logs for the week. What do you think led you to use or not to use ideas from the professional development event? Do you think there was a direct connection between the professional development and your class, or did you have to find ways to make it relevant? What else do you notice about the relationship between the professional development event and your teaching?

Activity 24: A Course Book Page We Love/Hate

Connections to research: Tsui points out that in any community, knowledge is distributed among the participants. This is true in classrooms. Although we usually consider the teacher the 'expert' in the classroom, learners also have important knowledge and perspectives that can contribute to the group learning and to the teacher's understanding of the classroom.

Materials

Your course book

Procedure

1. If you use a course book regularly with your class, ask students to think for homework what their favourite/least favourite unit/page/ activity in the book is and why. Do this homework yourself too.

2. If you have a shy group, do this next step yourself first. Otherwise, invite a different pair or group of students each time to tell the class about the section they have chosen and why the section is their most/least favourite.

3. If you think it will be difficult for your students to give reasons for their opinions apart from the obvious, 'Well, because I just (don't) like it', you might like to provide a checklist of possible reasons. These could include ideas such as:

    I don't like the pictures, the grammar is too hard, too many new words, I don't understand what we have to do, I really like the topic, this is useful, I've been to the place in the photo!

4. It is very important for you and the class to accept what the student chosen puts forward and not to praise, blame, or argue with the student over their choice or their reason. After all, many students will get their chance to express themselves on the topic.

5. If many in the class dislike a particular section, you can all discuss interesting ways of dealing with the offending unit.

Extensions and Variations

a) If you like to ring the changes and try different ways of doing things in your lessons—for example, sometimes using a course book, sometimes using home-made materials, sometimes using new technologies, at other times using no materials at all, sometimes presenting new information yourself, other times letting students find it out for themselves—then the discussion can be on lesson types rather than course book pages.

Make a point of signposting the different types of lessons you use as you teach through a term. Then, towards the end of term, take a moment with students to generate examples of the types of lessons they have experienced with you, so that it gets them thinking. Ask students to think for homework what their favourite and least favourite types of lesson were. Do this homework yourself too. If you do this via dialogue journals (see Activity 27), you can simply read your student journal entries and answer them individually. If, instead, you do the activity in class and have a shy group, start with yourself. Otherwise, invite a different student each time to tell the class about the lesson type they have chosen and why it was their most/least favourite.

Think about how you can use this information. It might help you to make a note of the likes and dislikes so that you can consider what they tell you about your students and about your teaching. You are likely to learn all sorts of surprising things from students, such as the importance of colour in a course book, or of success or praise to them. Students are likely to be surprised, too, to find that teachers also have their pet hates in a course book or lesson type.

b) If your class is very large, students can work in groups or pairs to discuss opinions and decide on one to put forward to the whole group.

c) Consider how this kind of openness with students is similar or different to the way you would have handled a problematic issue with a course book or lesson type when you were in your first year as a teacher.

Further Reading

Woodward, T. (2001). *Planning lessons and courses*. Cambridge: Cambridge University Press. (see especially pp. 145–160 and Chapter 4).

Activity 25: They Keep Getting Younger!

Connections to research: Huberman comments that those of us who stay in one post as we age start to notice a relational distance between us and our students. How can we deal with this?

Materials

None

Procedure

1. Either on your own or with colleagues, think about the fact that most students/pupils entering their class in your institution in, say, 2018 will have been born in the year 1998. These students are therefore not surprised that they can pay for a coffee with their phone, read a book on a tiny electronic screen and know what news is trending without ever reading a newspaper, listening to the radio, or watching the TV news.

2. Next, make a list such as the following.

    These students . . .

    > *Know that The Green Giant is Shrek and not a big guy picking veggies*

    > *Have never used a card index to find a book in the library*

    > *Have never seen a black and white TV*

    > *Have always known that Barbie is curvy and has a job . . .*

    Older members of staff can be a good resource for items on this list that attempts to highlight, through humour, the many changes in life that have happened since many of the teachers in your institution were born.

3. Keep the list near you throughout the term to remind you how different the mindset of your average class member is and also to

remind yourself that it is not the students' fault—and that teachers can look pretty weird to students, too.

Extensions and Variations

Other lists can be useful too. For example, you can make a list entitled, 'What do my students do in class that I wouldn't do? And 'What do my students *not* do in class that I would do?' Having made these lists, consider how this makes you feel and what you plan to do about it!

Further Reading

This idea is based on and some of the examples are drawn from the Beloit College, Wisconsin, USA 'Mindset List' (see www.beloit.edu/mindset/previouslists/2018/).

Activity 26: How Do I See My Students?

Connections to research: Lortie's term 'apprenticeship of observation' has often been interpreted as 'we teach the way we were taught'. A more accurate interpretation is that we teach *in relation to* how we were taught in both positive and negative ways, adopting some and rejecting other aspects of our education. Because the apprenticeship is intuitive and imitative, rather than analytical, we may not be aware of values and assumptions that influence our teaching. The example given in Part 1 (page 47) was of a math class in which the teacher only called on the boys, never the girls. What kinds of messages about girls' math capacity were unconsciously received in that class? This activity is designed to help you uncover potential biases you may have, but not be aware of.

Materials

Large sheets of paper

Procedure

1. Choose a class that you teach in which there is diversity of some
   kind, whether it be language, culture, level, educational background,
   age, and so on. On a sheet of paper, draw figures to represent the
   students in the class (these can be stick figures or simple faces) and
   write a student's name under each one.

2. Look at the students and choose the two you think are most
   likely to succeed in their studies and the two whom you think
   are least likely to succeed. This is clearly an exercise in judgment, which you may find difficult. However, most of us, if
   pressed, could say who our 'stars' are and who our 'concerns'
   are in a class we teach.

3. For each person, list at least five reasons that you have chosen
   them as most or least likely to succeed. Give specific examples/
   evidence for each reason.

4. Read through the reasons and the evidence. Do you notice any
   patterns in your responses? What do they show you about what
   you value or look for? How is your relationship or attitude towards
   the students evident in what you have written? Where do you think
   these values and attitudes come from?

Activity 27: Dialogue Journals

Connections to research: One of Lortie's findings was that
teaching is a balancing act between instructional goals (i.e. what
we want students to learn) and relational work, which involves
establishing rapport with them and helping them to manage their
learning. Dialogue journals are a wonderful means of getting to
know our students and how they think about their experiences in
the classroom.

From Implications to Application

Materials

The activity below uses a set of notebooks, one for each student in a class, since this gives maximum confidentiality. But use an online platform and set up individual threads if you prefer or encourage students to adapt use of their Personal Learning Environments (PLEs) to the idea below.

Procedure

1. Each student has their own notebook and writes their name and yours on the front cover (e.g. 'Gabi/Tessa'). They can customise their notebooks with stickers and drawings too if they wish.

2. Write a letter to your students, starting:

> Dear Students,
>
> The idea of this notebook is that we write letters to each other. The letters are private and give you practice writing in English about things that interest you. For example . . .

In this way you explain the idea of the notebook. Suggest how they can answer your letter when they write in the notebook below your entry (see below for ideas to prompt this). Finish the letter as you normally would (e.g. 'Best wishes' and sign your name).

3. Stick a copy of this starter letter in each student's notebook as the first entry.

4. Set a time for students to answer your letter. Perhaps set aside five minutes at the end of a lesson or set the letter writing for homework.

5. Each student writes an answer to your letter in their notebook, under your entry. They should start with 'Dear' and the name they usually call you by, and finish appropriately with, for example, 'All the best' and sign their name.

6. They hand the notebook in. When you read the student entries, you may wish to address student language errors or not. If you choose to, you can do so in different ways. For example, you can decide not to correct their English by writing on their letters or using a red pen but answer their letter as you would a letter from a friend, starting with Dear (First name), writing honestly and with real content, and asking questions that they can use in their next reply in the notebook. You can deal with any maladroit phrases in their letter by paraphrasing in your reply, as in this example. Student writes, 'Then I have gone home.' Teacher writes in reply letter, 'So, then you went home. I see!'

7. The notebooks, which can be placed in envelopes for even greater privacy if preferred, travel back and forth between each student and the teacher. To prevent overload of work for the teacher, you can make dialogue journals optional. Usually about a third of a class will really get into them. Or set the dialogue journals as homework for different students on different days.

8. You can suggest topics for the students to write about until they have become confident in reading and writing in English and start to venture topics of their own. See below for topic suggestions.

9. Make your own replies natural and interesting so that students will enjoy learning about you too.

10. In terms of your development as a teacher, consider what you have learned about your students that can help you adjust your teaching to meet their needs. What have you learned about or from your students that was unexpected or surprising? How did it change your thinking or practice? How did the way you respond to the entries over time change? Did you respond to different students in different ways? What do you think accounts for the differences or changes?

Extensions and Variations

The idea above involves the use of the epistolary or letter-writing form. Other forms are also possible.

From Implications to Application

a) Depending on the language level of your students, you can ask them to write just one or two short sentences, building up from there to longer sentences, then to more of them, and then to paragraphs.

b) You can give starter phrases such as, 'When I was younger I used to . . .' and ask students to start three sentences that are true about themselves in the same way.

c) You can set a topic to support work done in class—for example:

'What did you do last weekend?' (Past Simple)

'What do you usually do in the mornings before school?' (Present Simple)

'Ask me three questions starting with the letters *Wh*.' (Wh Question practice)

d) You can give a weekly prompt for students to write about and give a short informal reply.

e) You can leave the student free to write about what she likes.

f) You can use the dialogue journals to find out more about your students, their daily lives, or their grasp of lesson content.

g) You can ask them which words from a vocabulary lesson they think they will remember and which they think they will forget.

h) You can sound them out about what kind of materials and lessons they prefer, ask them about their hobbies, and so on.

Further Reading

Dudeney, G., Hockly, N., & Pegrum, M. (2013). *Digital literacies*. Harlow, UK: Pearson (see p. 30).

Peyton, J., & Reed, L. (1990). *Dialogue journal writing with nonnative English speakers: A handbook for teachers*. Alexandria, VA: TESOL.

Peyton, J., & Staton, J. (Eds.). (1991). *Writing our lives: Reflections on dialogue journal writing with adults learning English*. Englewood Cliffs, NJ: Regents Prentice Hall and Center for Applied Linguistics.

Peyton, J., & Staton, J. (1993). *Dialogue journals in the multilingual classroom: Building language fluency and writing skills through written interaction*. Norwood, NJ: Ablex.

Woodward, T. (2001). *Planning lessons and courses*. Cambridge: Cambridge University Press.

Activity 28: Building Case Studies

Connections to research: Building a case study, such as the one described below, allows us to stand back and explore some aspect of our practice from different perspectives and gain fresh insights that might help us reframe it. This is very much in keeping with Tsui's notion of problematising.

Materials

None

Procedure

1. Choose an issue that you would like to work on. It could be, for example, dealing with mixed ability classes, or getting on with a difficult colleague, or dealing with a rambunctious student. It could be from the third column, 'Things I feel less comfortable with in my work at the moment' from *Where Do I Want to Go Next?* (Activity 37).

2. Think of a few instances over your working life that have pinpointed this puzzle for you. Then write a couple of paragraphs as a short case study. Include details of the sort of thing that has happened and continues to happen in real life but don't mention any particular classes, students, or staff by name.

3. Show the case study to someone else and ask them to check that there is enough information in the text for them to understand your issue. (See example text below.)

From Implications to Application

4. If they need to ask questions to clarify things, then use their remarks to help you make the case study better. Once your case study is clear, share it with someone and ask them the following questions:

    •   *How many problems/issues/puzzles do you see?*

    •   *What possible solutions do you see?*

5. If you do this orally, listen to them well as they answer the questions, trying very hard not to interrupt or judge them for what they say; instead, when they have finished commenting, thank them for their insights. If you know you will have trouble with this part, ask the helper to write their answers instead!

6. If you work on your own without colleagues, conduct an Internet search on the topic and note down all the ideas you come across again without censoring any.

Example text (before colleague questions):

A very advanced student in my class asked me a tricky language question right in the middle of our doing something else. I thought about it for a second and, realizing it was not a black-and-white, yes-or-no issue, said I'd like to give her an answer the next day. I explained that if I gave her a quick answer on the spot it might not be a good or complete one.

The student looked nettled. She said I was a 'Native Speaker' and so should know my own language especially as it was my job.

I wrote the language query down, together with the student's name, and promised to deal with it next day. Later that day I thought, read a usage book and discussed the query with colleagues. I then wrote my various thoughts on a piece of paper. Next day, not wanting to take up too much class time, I gave the written thoughts on the language point to the student. She scanned it briefly, declared that it was wishy-washy and unhelpful, left the paper on her desk, and then left the room.

Dear Colleague,

Is this text clear enough for you to understand the issue in the case study or does it need more detail?

Thanks!

Tessa

See also the discussion of the Critical Friends protocol in Part 4.

Further Reading

Tripp, D. (2012). *Critical incidents in teaching: Developing professional judgment.* London: Routledge.

Activity 29: Freirean Problem Posing

Connections to research: This activity relates to Tsui's discussion of problematising and being able to reframe one's practice based on other perspectives. It uses the problem-posing sequence (Wallerstein, 1982) that is an adaptation of Paulo Freire's approach in his work with literacy. Freire, an educator who developed an approach to native language literacy for rural peoples in the north of Brazil, considered education to be a process of dialogue among equals, not what he called a 'banking model' in which the teacher's primary role is to 'deposit' information in students. 'Problem posing' is distinct from problem-solving, which sometimes presumes there is one right answer.

Materials

This will depend on how the problem is represented (see below).

Procedure

1. Choose something from your practice that has been problematic and that you would like to understand better. For example, it could be

student apathy, your feelings about the curriculum, your relationship with a supervisor. Think of an analogous situation that does not involve you directly—this is so you can be somewhat detached and gain a broader perspective. The situation can be taken from outside of the classroom or school setting. For example, if you are concerned about your relationship with a supervisor, a similar or analogous situation would be one in which there is a power differential between people. These could be ones that involve students and their teacher, or children and their parents. (See the example in the next step.)

2. Identify or create an artefact (e.g. a picture, cartoon, advertisement) or compose a short narrative, a dialogue, or scenario that captures the situation. This is called a 'code', as it acts as a shorthand to represent the situation. For example, the following dialogue (a true story) between a Kindergarten teacher and one of her young students could be used as a code for a relationship with a supervisor:

Teacher: Now, I want all of you to cooperate. Do you know what that means?

[Students raise their hands; the teacher calls on Sarah.]

Sarah: Yes, it means do as you say.

3. Answer the following questions about the artefact, narrative, dialogue, or scenario. The questions should be answered in the order in which they appear as each answer builds on the previous one.

    If you are working individually, write out your responses to the questions. If you are working with a colleague, talk through your answers.

Describe:

- *Who are the people involved?*

- *What is the situation about?*

- *How do you think each person feels?*

(The purpose of this step is to bring out multiple perspectives so that participants see the issue from the point of view of each person.)

Define the problem:

- *What is the problem here?*

- *Is there more than one?*

Relate it to individual experience:

- *Has anything like this ever happened to you?*

- *Do you ever feel like any of the people in the case?*

Analyse root causes:

- *Where did this problem come from?*

- *Why does it exist? Who created this situation?*

(The purpose of this step is to look for the broader social/historical context.)

Plan for action:

- *What can the people involved do?*

- *What can you do?*

Figure out strategies. What are the consequences of each?

Further Reading

Wallerstein, N. (1982). *Language and culture in conflict: Problem-posing in the ESL classroom*. Reading, MA: Addison-Wesley.

Activity 30: Teaching Bump

Connections to research: Understanding one's students is an important part of what Lortie calls the relational work of teaching. As

> described in Part 1, page 12, this involves "1) [producing] affection
> and respect from students; . . . 2) [getting] work out of students; 3)
> [and] . . . winning student compliance and discipline" (p. 117). Yet we
> have all had experiences of miscommunication or misunderstandings
> with students, and even antagonism from them. This activity helps to
> see those experiences from the student's point of view.

Materials

Large sheets of paper (A3 or 11 1/2 × 14)

Procedure

Note: This activity is based on something called a culture bump (Archer,
1986). Culture bumps are incidents in which you have an interaction
with someone from another culture (or subculture) in which you have
feelings of discomfort, strangeness, or miscommunication with the other
person. Sometimes it is a feeling of mild discomfort that is hard to even
identify. Other times the feelings are much more obvious and result in a
breakdown between you and the other person. As with any bump, there
is always a mixture of individual/cultural factors—and it may be hard to
tease out what is what.

1. Identify an incident in which you had an interaction with a student or
   students in which you had feelings of discomfort or a miscommunication with the student(s).

2. Describe (in writing) the interaction as clearly and objectively as you
   can. In other words, write a narrative of what happened, without any
   interpretation.

3. Now rewrite the narrative from your perspective in first person and
   include how you felt and how you interpreted the situation.

4. Now rewrite the narrative from the perspective of the other person,
   also in first person, and include how they felt and interpreted the

situation. The purpose of writing it from the perspective of the other person is to try to enter their world and to see it from their viewpoint.

5. Step back and analyse the source of the problem. If you do this with a colleague or colleagues, explain your analysis and also what you've learned about yourself. If you are working alone, write out the analysis and then conclude it with what you learned about yourself.

Further Reading

Archer, C. (1986). Culture bump and beyond. In J. M. Valdes (Ed.), *Culture bound*: *Bridging the cultural gap in language teaching* (pp. 170–178). Cambridge: Cambridge University Press.

Activity 31: From Tactics to Beliefs: The Four-Column Analysis

Connections to research: Huberman encouraged teachers to look back over a career and to divide it up into phases. This activity encourages us to do the same thing at the level of the individual lesson, thus investigating what activities, sequences, chunks, and phases we use; why we use them; and whether there is coherence between what we feel and believe, what we actually do, and how others see our work. As teachers, we spend quite a lot of our time looking forward to future lessons and much less time thinking back through a lesson we have just taught.

Materials

A large sheet of paper oriented to landscape with four columns labelled:

Steps	Phases	Assumptions (or Beliefs)	Archaeology

You may wish, instead, to make four circles or strips with each of the labels, depending on how you prefer to visualise things.

From Implications to Application

Procedure

Note: This activity can be done alone or with a colleague.

1. Choose a lesson you have taught.

2. Fill in the 'Steps' column. Try to remember the individual steps of the lesson without looking directly at your source material (e.g. the lesson plan). Note down the steps of the lesson.

    (Rationale: As teachers, we spend a lot of our time looking forward to future lessons and much less time thinking back through a lesson we have just taught. So we are usually practised at pre-paration but not post-paration. Looking back is good memory training. It forces us to look at all that went on and not just the bits that seemed most important, most right, or most wrong.)

3. Fill in the 'Phases' column. Look at all the steps you noted in the first column. Perhaps you have numbered them 1–10. See if you would like to clump some of them together into phases with nicknames (e.g. 'Warm up', 'Getting into the topic', 'Getting into the language patterns', 'Practice phase', 'Setting homework and leave taking').

    (Rationale: You may find that you very often use similar phases in your lessons and in similar orders. If you are working with a colleague, you might be intrigued to see that they structure their lessons in identical or very different ways to yours.)

4. Fill in the 'Assumptions' (or 'Beliefs') column. Look at the individual steps and phases listed in columns one and two and try to get to the assumptions and beliefs behind them.

    (Rationale: If working with a colleague, ask whether they see things differently from you. For example, you might believe that having music playing relaxes students but your colleague might pick up that it all depends on the type of music, type of student, and the volume!)

5. Fill in the 'Archaeology' column. This column could also be headed 'When, how, and why did I learn this way of working?' Try to remember where an activity or a sequence or the idea for a phase came from. How did you learn it?

    (Rationale: This helps us to understand how we teachers learn, where we get our repertoires from, and in what situations we are most likely to pick up new ways of working. We begin to dig out the history of our own improvement as teachers. So, we may see that we learn most from people or from books or from a Personal Learning Environment (PLE).)

Variations

Compare your notes in Column 1, 'Steps', with the lesson plan or other source material, to see what you remembered and what you forgot and to consider why you remembered the bits you did. This prompts a more realistic and detailed reflection on or discussion of a lesson or session than when just remembering the things that stand out most immediately and vividly.

Further Reading

Woodward, T. (2001). *Planning lessons and courses*. Cambridge: Cambridge University Press (see pp. 8–14).

Activity 32: Constraints and Resources of My Teaching Context

Connections to research: Both Tsui and Lortie discuss the importance of context in shaping a teacher's practice and development. Tsui's study highlighted the way in which each teacher related to her context. She found that an expert teacher is able to identify constraints that she feels are important to address and figure out how to 'transcend' them.

From Implications to Application

Materials

Large sheets of paper (A3 or 11 1/2 × 14)

Procedure

1. Write an introduction to your context: where you teach and what the physical space is like, how it is organised, and how it is used; who your colleagues and administrators are, especially those with whom you interact; who your students are—numbers, cultural and educational backgrounds, proficiency levels, ages, and so on; the materials that you use and where you get them from; what the timetable is and how your own teaching fits within it; what your classroom(s) is/are like.

    Our contexts of work are complex, dynamic environments. Each context provides resources that we can use to facilitate our work, as well as constraints that we have to adapt to or overcome. These resources and constraints are both tangible (e.g. materials) and intangible (e.g. attitudes). They are both human (e.g. your students, colleagues, parents, administrators) and non-human (e.g. equipment, furniture, classroom space). Many features of our contexts are both constraints and resources. For example, a timetable is a resource because it helps to organise our time and it is also a constraint because it limits our time.

2. On a sheet of paper create a Venn diagram. This is a diagram in which two circles overlap, so that there are three spaces: the left part of one circle, the middle part where both circles overlap, and the right part of the other circle. Label the left part 'resources' and the right part 'constraints' (as in Figure 2.1).

3. Review the description you wrote in Step 1 and use it to help you identify the resources of your context. What do you see as the resources of your context? Fill in the 'resources' part of the diagram.

4. Review the description again, this time to help you identify the constraints of your context.

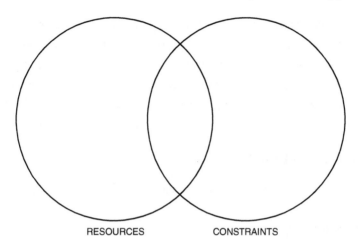

RESOURCES   CONSTRAINTS

Figure 2.1 Activity 32: Venn Diagram

What are the constraints of your context? Fill in the 'constraints' part of the diagram.

5. Spend some time considering what you've written. What do you notice? Are there items in both circles? Move them to the overlapping part. Is one list longer than the other? Why do you think that is so? If you had made a similar list at an earlier point in your career, how would it be the same? How would it be different?

6. Transcending a constraint involves creativity and determination or a 'can-do' mindset. Not all constraints are worth addressing and some may be ones you can't address, at least individually. Identify a constraint that you want to address because it limits something that is important to the success of your students. For example, one of the authors (Kathleen) worked with a teacher who identified the number of students (over 60) as a constraint that limited students' opportunities to speak in class. The expert teacher in Tsui's study identified the lack of English except in the classroom as a constraint for her students.

7. Brainstorm at least three ways you can address this constraint. Then choose the one that seems most sensible to you. For example, the teacher who identified the size of her class as a constraint divided the

class into teams. Each team chose a name. The teacher designed communication activities that could be conducted within these teams. The teacher in Tsui's study created an English-rich classroom by bringing realia and authentic materials into the class; by posting the students' English work on a class bulletin board; and by creating tasks for students to do outside of the classroom that used English.

Extensions and Variations

Do Step 5 with a colleague or colleagues.

Further Reading

Graves, K. (2000) *Designing language courses: A guide for teachers*. Boston: Heinle Cengage (See Chapter 2).

Activity 33: Describing My Work

Connections to research: Lortie writes about how teachers' work looks (and sounds) very different to teachers and their colleagues than it does the public at large. This separation of views is often evident in how we use jargon terms and acronyms as 'insider' talk to describe what we do.

Materials

None

Procedure

1. Draft three to five sentences describing the work you do (e.g. 'I teach at an elementary school in Greece. My students are from 5 to 10 years old. I teach them English through Art. I work with a TA.').

2. Underline the terms you think teachers in other settings may not understand or relate to.

3. Look at the following list of acronyms, initials, adjectives, nouns, and terms used to describe different types of teachers at different stages of their careers. Decide which ones apply to you and which don't:

		Working with . . . students/pupils	In a . . . school	On . . .
PRESET (Pre service teacher)	Intern	primary	private	CLIL (Content and Language Integrated Learning)
INSET (In-service teacher)	Mentee	secondary	government	ESP (English for Special Purposes)
TA (Teaching Assistant) Probationary	Mentor	tertiary/university	religious	EAP (English for Academic Purposes)
Rookie	Trainee	adult	special school	General English
Inexperienced	Bi-lingual teacher			
Experienced	Multi-lingual teacher			
Veteran	Mono-lingual teacher			
	Trainer			

From Implications to Application

4. Then draft a mini description of yourself starting with the words:

    'I am a . . .' and *'I'm not a . . .'*

5. Imagine you are attending an international ELT (English Language Teaching) conference and, mingling with classmates or co-workers, practice introducing yourself using your mini description.

Activity 34: Half-Scripted Interviews

Connections to research: Tsui suggests problematising aspects of our teaching that we take for granted. Another way of thinking of this is 'to make the familiar strange'. This playful activity helps you to consider different attitudes towards discipline in the classroom.

Materials

The half-scripted interviews below

Procedure

1. Work with a colleague. One of you, A, starts as the interviewer for the first interview, asking the questions on Sheet One below and giving B time to think and answer after each question. A can add more questions as they go along if they like. B will not know very much about themselves in role at the start of the interview, but things will become clearer as the interview unfolds. The idea for B is NOT to answer the questions truthfully as him- or herself but to enjoy answering imaginatively and in role!

2. Next it is B's turn to be the interviewer using the (different) questions on Sheet Two below. A should now enjoy answering the questions according to their whim and fancy and in role, as that role becomes clear to them.

3. The idea of this activity is to have some fun, which we too often overlook in teacher development. Afterwards, we suggest

discussing what it felt like to 'be' teacher A or teacher B. What are the merits and demerits of the teacher attitudes in the interviews?

Sheet One: Interviewing the Winner of 'The Strictest Teacher of the Year' Award

Interviewer Questions

- Thank you for granting this interview. Readers of our magazine, *Teaching Today*, will be very interested to read what the best thing is, in your opinion, about being judged 'The Strictest Teacher of the Year'?

- Were you surprised by this award? I mean, did you decide to have a strict regime in class and, if so, why?

- What do you plan to do with the £10,000 prize you have won?

- Before you were a teacher, you were a sergeant major in the army. I've heard that you decided to leave the army for a couple of specific reasons. What were they?

- Of course, there are some army skills that transfer to the language classroom. Can you list them?

- Did you model yourself on any particularly strict teacher you had when you were a student?

- Also, was there a particularly soft or lax teacher you didn't want to be like?

- In what ways was that teacher lax?

- We understand that your students complained to the head of your school about this accolade. Why was that, do you think?

- By the way, your recent autobiography is selling very well. What was the title again?

- And the subtitle?

- Which bit did you enjoy writing most and why?

From Implications to Application

- And I understand you are starting a new line of merchandise selling online. What sort of things are you selling?

- What is your brand?

- What sort of teachers are buying from you?

- Well, coming back to the classroom, can you tell us a few things about the worst student you have ever had?

- And a few things about the best?

- What four things made you like that student?

- And finally, what do you think the future holds for you now, in going back to your students? Your colleagues? Your Head of school?

Well, thank you very much for giving up your time for this interview!

Sheet Two: Interviewing the Person Who Came Last in the Competition for 'The Strictest Teacher of the Year' Award

Interviewer Questions

- It's very good of you to grant this interview with our magazine, *Teaching Today*. And all commiserations for coming last in the competition.

- Were you surprised at coming last? Is this embarrassing to you, or is this a good thing, in your opinion?

- What do you plan to do with the stuffed rabbit booby prize you have won?

- Before you were a teacher, you were a child psychologist. I've heard that you decided to leave the scientific community for a couple of specific reasons. What were they?

- Of course, there are some aspects of child psychology that transfer to the language classroom. Can you list them?

- We understand that your students complained to the head of your school about your being given a booby prize. Why was that, do you think?

- I know that the students banded together to get you a reward. What did they get you?

- I understand you have a very popular web site for teachers. What's on it?

- And you are running a campaign to make some changes in education. What are they?

- What sort of teachers join in with your blogs and your campaign?

- Well, coming back to the classroom, can you tell us a few things about the most challenging student you have ever had?

- Do you think teachers should expect to like all their students?

- You are known for having several passions and hobbies outside school. What are they?

- Do you bring them into school at all?

- And, finally, what do you think the future holds for you now, in going back to your students? Your colleagues? Your head of school?

Well, thank you very much. That was most interesting!

Further Reading

For half scripted interviews with language learners, see Woodward, T., & Lindstromberg, S. (2014). *Something to say*. Rum, Austria: Helbling Languages.

Activity 35: Writing an Op-Ed

Connections to research: Lortie's work reveals how little people who are not teachers understand about the nature of the work of teachers. This activity is designed to help you explain something that matters to you about education so that people can better understand it.

From Implications to Application

Materials

Large sheets of paper

Procedure

1. Op-ed is short for 'opinion-editorial'. It is usually a short essay in a
    newspaper or journal that has a strong point of view on a current
    issue—usually an issue that has sparked controversy. The writer
    explores different sides of the issue and then aims to persuade the
    reader of his or her opinion and what can be done about the issue
    by using a combination of anecdotes and data. For example, one
    ESL teacher in the US wrote an op-ed about why collaboration
    between ESL specialist teachers and subject area teachers is the
    best way to help English language learners succeed in public sector
    schools.

    The first step is to read at least two op-eds—editorials in newspa-
    pers that can be found online (or a print newspaper)—and make
    notes on the strategies you think the author uses to make his or her
    point. Some things to consider:

    What did the author do to try to persuade you of his or her point
    of view? For example, did the author explain the issue clearly? Did
    she or he provide convincing evidence? Did she or he use personal
    experience? Did the title make you want to read it?

    Was there anything that put you off? What was it? Why did it put
    you off?

    What should the author have done to better persuade you?

2. Choose an issue that is important to you in your practice, but
    that may be new to, misunderstood by, or overly simplified by the
    non-teaching public. Some examples: why it is a bad (or good) idea
    to mandate language education in early grades; whether you can
    teach English just because you grew up speaking it; why asking
    questions around the class one-by-one is not a great idea; why

multiple forms of assessment are better than standardised tests to measure achievement.

3. Write a draft of an op-ed in which you describe the issue and what can be done about it. Use your notes from Step 1 and the following list of tips. The tips are adapted from Duke University's Office of News and Communications (2017):

    1   Shorter is better (750 words is a good limit)

    2   Make a simple point well and up-front

    3   Tell readers why they should care

    4   Offer specific recommendations

    5   Embrace your personal voice

    6   Use short sentences and paragraphs

    7   Use the active voice

    8   Acknowledge the other side

    9   Make your beginning a hook and your ending zing

    10 Relax and have fun with the writing!

4. Give the draft to one or two non-teaching friends and one or two colleagues to read and ask them for suggestions for how to improve it.

5. Write a final draft.

6. Consider publishing the op-ed in a local print or online publication or blog.

Further Reading

For more detail on these tips for writing op-ed pieces, see Duke University's Office of News and Communications. (2017). Retrieved from https://styleguide.duke.edu/toolkits/writing-media/how-to-write-an-op-ed-article/

Activity 36: Two Maps of Professional Learning

Connections to research: The *Learning4Teaching* Project has examined how teachers make sense of and transform input from professional development events to work in their classrooms. This view contrasts with the generally held view of professional development as 'causing' changes in classroom teaching. Both are views of how teachers learn from professional development. Each one may be valid, so it is worth comparing them, using your own experience as a lens.

Materials

Table 2.5 and Figure 2.2 (which are based on Table 1.4 and the same as Figure 1.1 from Part 1).

NOTE: *In this activity, you use Table 2.5 and Figure 2.2 as two possible 'maps' of professional learning. As with any map, each one highlights certain features of the landscape and downplays or omits others. To explore the differences, you are asked to use your experience to identify, consider, and challenge the elements in each map. The task can be abstract, but think of it as using a road map to figure out where you are, where you've been, and where you may be headed.*

Procedure

1. Talking through each map: Look over Table 2.5 and Figure 2.2 one at a time. Thinking of each as a map of how teachers learn from professional development:

    •   Identify and talk through the features of each map in your own words. For example, 'I think the left-hand box in Table 2.5 is saying that when you do professional development, an

Table 2.5 The premises underlying the design of the *Learning4Teaching* Project

	Professional learning→	Teacher participation→		Classroom use
PREMISE	A given professional development activity offers an opportunity to learn	Participating and making sense of an opportunity to learn influences	Individual uptake of ideas and practices, which influences	Using the ideas and practices in the classroom

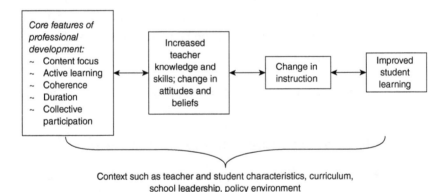

Figure 2.2 "Conceptual framework for studying the effects of professional development on teachers and students" (Desimone, 2009, p. 185)

opportunity is created to learn something. But it isn't saying what you learn, or even that you do learn something . . .'

• Now look at the connections between each of the four boxes in each map. *How does what is supposed to happen in each box relate/connect to the boxes on each side?*

From Implications to Application

2. Comparing the maps: They each have four boxes. Working from left to right on each, compare each set of boxes. (A) *How are the two similar?* (B) *How are they different?*

    It can help to set up a chart like the one below:

	Box 1	Box 2	Box 3	Box 4
A: similar				
B: different				

3. Using your experience: Think of a recent professional development event that you took part in. If you are doing this with fellow teachers, it could be the same event, but it can be more useful for each person to think of a different event.

    - Review what happened. Talk through the event from start to finish.

    - Choose either the table or the figure to 'map' the event.

        - Start with what was supposed to happen—how the event was supposed to play out. *What did those who provided the event think was the focus? What did they think you were supposed to learn?*

        - Then think about your perspective: *What did you take from the event? How did you use what you learned?*

        - Recognising that there are bound to be differences in perspective between the providers and participants in a professional development event, *which figure is a better 'map' of your experience of the event?*

- Discuss with your colleagues which of the maps seems to more fully capture your experiences of learning from professional development.

Extensions and Variations

You can also start with Table 2.5 and Figure 2.2 themselves and brainstorm examples of professional development events that could illustrate each of the maps. Consider questions like *How does the event 'fit' this diagram? What was the event supposed to accomplish? How did it go for you? What were some of the advantages and disadvantages?*

———————————

In Section C, we have encouraged you to consider where you are in your professional life now, what you know how to do, what you still need to know, and how you feel about your students and your work. You have considered, among others, the issues in teaching that matter to you now and how you make sense of them, what you are good at and the challenges you face, how you use theory to inform your practice, what you can learn from colleagues and students, your relationship to your teaching context, and how you can stay motivated to expand your professional horizons. In the next section, we turn to the future.

D. Where Am I Headed?

Alice:	Would you tell me, please, which way I ought to go from here?
Cheshire Cat:	That depends a good deal on where you want to get to.
Alice:	I don't much care where.
Cheshire Cat:	Then it doesn't matter which way you go . . .
Alice:	. . . so long as I get somewhere.

From Implications to Application

Cheshire Cat;   Oh, you're sure to do that, if you only walk long enough.

(Carroll, 1865)

The activities in Section D aim to help you get a second wind, to gain the motivation to continue learning about teaching, and to figure out what you want to learn next as a teacher.

Activity 37: *Where Do I Want to Go Next?*
Activity 38: *A 'Good' Teacher Is . . .*
Activity 39: *How Do I Grow a Teacher Learning Technique?*
Activity 40: *What's in My Teaching Suitcase?*
Activity 41: *Who Is My 'Go To Person'?*
Activity 42: *Who I Could Become*
Activity 43: *Talking to My (Other) Self*
Activity 44: *Mapping the Future*
Activity 45: *From Known to New*
Activity 46: *An Eddy in the River*
Activity 47: *Graphic Organiser for Teacher Training and Development*
Activity 48: *I Plan, You Teach. You Plan, I Teach.*
Activity 49: *Finding Balance Then Staying Interested*
Activity 50: *Breaking Rules*
Activity 51: *Moving On: Collecting or Throwing Away?*
Activity 52: *Moving On, Heading Out*

Some of the questions to consider are:

- What's next for me?

- How will I know that I have learned what I want or need to learn? What will satisfy my learning at this point?

- Can I move between stages, skip stages, or 'inhabit' more than one stage at once?

- What is the 'edge' of my competence where I want to push myself to grow?

Activity 37: Where Do I Want to Go Next?

Connections to research: Drawing from his interviews with teachers, Lortie described teaching as a 'one-step career', by which he referred to the public perception that a teacher's job remains fairly stable, constant, and unchanging. Although this is clearly a misperception, we often can get the impression from public discourse about teaching that the basic work never changes.

Materials

A sheet of paper

Procedure

1. Divide a sheet of paper into three columns. Title the left hand column, 'Things I found difficult when I first started teaching'; the middle column, 'Things I feel comfortable with in my work now'; and the right hand column, 'Things I feel less comfortable with in my work at the moment'.

2. Think about the teaching you've done and are doing now and make notes under each column. You can include any area of your work: content knowledge, practical skills, social relations, attitudes, employment conditions, or anything else that comes to mind.

3. When you have filled in the table, read through what you've written in the right hand column, 'Things I feel less comfortable with in my work at the moment', and choose one of the topics there as an issue to work on next.

4. Talk to a colleague about the issue or research it by looking at teacher web sites on the Internet or by reading through some teaching periodicals.

5. Write down three things you can do to pursue learning in that area. Decide what you will try to achieve, how, and by when.

Activity 38: A 'Good' Teacher Is . . .

Connections to research: According to Tsui, one of the critical differences between a 'non-expert experienced teacher' and an 'expert' teacher is the way each relates to context. This activity gets you to think about how you relate to your context by reflecting on what is valued in a teacher and why.

Materials

None

Procedure

1. Write ten sentences using the starter phrase, 'In my setting, a 'good' teacher is considered to . . .' and then the following verbs: *be, do, know, have* . . .

2. Next, continue with some writing that starts, 'The reasons for this are . . .'

3. Then continue by writing sentences starting, 'The way I feel about this is . . .'

4. Consider whether you are happy with the way you feel about the idea of a 'good' teacher in your setting.

Activity 39: How Do I Grow a Teacher Learning Technique?

Connections to research: Lortie's study identified the tension between autonomy—that each teacher is responsible for their *own* class—and isolation—but they *teach alone*. To break through this tension often requires teachers to organise professional relations with colleagues, to forego a bit of autonomy, in order to break the isolation and get another view on what is going on in their teaching.

Materials

None

Procedure

1. Take a form of teacher learning that you have found really useful in your career so far (e.g. peer observation). Consider how you undertook this at the start of your career.

   - *Perhaps you needed to learn just what there was to see when you watched someone teach?*

   - *Perhaps you consulted a list of the major components of a lesson, perhaps on an observation checklist given to you by a teacher trainer?*

   - *Perhaps you were able to tick off things that you noticed during the lesson such as board work or pair work or the number of open and closed questions asked by the teacher?*

2. Next, talk to more experienced, mid-career teachers and ask what sorts of things they notice when they do peer observation. Do they pick up new ways of doing known activities? Or new activities all together? Perhaps they see more detail in the same major components or instead get interested in other brand new categories such as professional judgment, when to step in to discipline a student, or how others broker the gender power balance in the class.

3. Next, consider the stance in Cosh (1998), where experienced teachers observing a peer at work in a class use the single question, 'What do I learn about my own teaching from watching you teach?' as the focus for their peer observation.

Further Reading

Cosh, J. (1998). Peer observation in higher education—a reflective approach. *Innovations in Education & Training International, 35*(2), 171–176.

Activity 40: What's in My Teaching Suitcase?

Connections to research: When we encounter a new teaching situation, whether it be new students, new content, or a new place of work, we become novices with respect to the element that changes. However, we have a store of teaching essentials that we travel with when we encounter that new element. As Tsui points out, being able to understand our teaching history can help us to draw on what we already know that can help us when we encounter the unfamiliar.

Materials

Sheet of paper for drawing

Procedure

This activity is designed to help you when you are headed into a new situation—teaching new content, teaching new students, teaching in a new place. In such a situation, you may feel that you are starting over as a novice teacher and forget how much you already know. The suitcase you will pack and unpack in this activity helps you to identify what you already know that you can rely on in the new situation.

A suitcase is something in which we pack what we will need at our destination(s). There are often certain things that we travel with because we know they are essential to our well-being in a new place or a place away from home. The contents of the suitcase are a metaphor for the teaching essentials we depend on.

1. Draw an outline of a suitcase. Divide it into four quadrants.

   Label the quadrants:

   learners   *learning*

   subject matter   *context*

These indicate the contents—what you are going to put in the suitcase.

2. Now, think about what you will put in each quadrant of the suitcase—these could be skills, concepts/viewpoints, activities, or attitudes. You can do this mentally or jot down a few notes.

    Take *learners*, for example. In your practice, what do you feel is important about learners? It could be that you know learners have lives outside of the classroom that impact what they do or how they are in the classroom (concept/viewpoint). And so you try not to judge individuals before you have gotten to know them (attitude). You have a repertoire of engaging getting-to-know-you activities to help everyone learn about each other and to set a welcoming tone for the class (activity).

    Take l*earning* as another example. An important idea for learning might be that the most effective way to learn something is to do it, not just know about it (concept/viewpoint). So you feel it is important to have activities in which learners *do* what they have been learning about, for example, when you have students create and conduct a survey on a focal topic (activity/skill). You encourage students to take risks and not be afraid of making mistakes (attitude).

    These skills, concepts/viewpoints, activities, or attitudes are the items you will pack in your suitcase to take with you to your new situation.

3. 'Pack' each item from Step 2 in the suitcase you drew by writing key words or drawing an image that captures it.

4. Project yourself into your new situation—with your new learners, or new content, or new environment. 'Unpack' each item in the suitcase by considering and making notes about how it can help you in your new situation or how you can adapt it.

From Implications to Application

Activity 41: Who Is My 'Go To Person'?

> **Connections to research**: Tsui makes the point that knowledge
> is both 'multiple' (we can't know everything in a given sphere) and
> 'distributed' (within an organisation like a school, different people
> have different kinds of knowledge). An expert teacher is good at
> collaborating with others and knowing who to consult to get the
> kind of information, ideas, or support she or he needs. This activity
> is aimed at preparing you to do this.

Materials

None

Procedure

1. Brainstorm a list of things that you want or need to learn at this point
   in your work. These could be specific skills; they could be information or knowledge about your students, your teaching situation, the
   content you are supposed to teach. They could also be attitudes
   that you feel you need to develop in order to be more effective and
   to sustain yourself in your work. Try to have at least three ideas in
   each of these categories.

2. For each of the items on your list, think about someone you know
   who does that thing (it may be someone in your immediate work
   environment; or someone you met at a conference, or someone
   you used to work with). Cast your net wide as you think about
   people.

3. Choose one item/thing and the person you have associated with it
   and draft a plan for how to be in touch with that person. It could be
   a phone call, an email, a cup of coffee.

4. Using the three sets of phrases or sentence starters below, draft
   your approach to the individual.

1. 'I'm finding in my current job that . . .'
2. 'I've been asked to . . . in my current job.'
3. 'One thing that I'm really working on in my current job is . . .'

4. 'I thought about you and your teaching in this connection because . . .'
5. 'When I think about people who do this well . . .'

6. 'I'd like to be in touch . . . have a phone conversation . . . get together. Would you be willing/interested?'

Activity 42: Who I Could Become

Connections to research: Huberman notes that there comes a time when we commit to teaching and turn our backs on other career choices previously entertained. But do we have to give up on those dreams entirely?

Materials

None

Procedure

1. Choose an occupation that you have always been intrigued by or interested in, perhaps your dream job (e.g. artist, singer, athlete, lawyer . . .).

2. List attributes of the job and make notes of your picture of the person who does the job, including their clothing, look, sound, the materials they use, the skills necessary, and also what the person usually does, eats, earns, and so on, in your mind's eye.

3. Do the same for your own job of teacher.

4. Next, make a third list of attributes that both jobs share. For example, both an artist and a teacher have to get to know their materials and to be creative in their work.

5. Finally, consider how the teacher could be more like the other person (e.g. the artist), and the other person (the artist) more like a teacher. How might you be able to bring some of the features of your dream job into your teaching? Don't discard apparently tiny or trivial features such as playing music at the start of class or dressing in slightly brighter clothes. Even tiny changes in routine can make us feel freer and more ourselves in our day-to-day work.

Further Reading

Fanselow, J. (1987). *Breaking rules: Generating and exploring alternatives in language teaching*. New York: Pearson. Also available, (2012). CreateSpace Independent Publishing Platform.
Woodward, T. (2011). *Thinking in the EFL class*. Rum, Austria: Helbling Languages.

Activity 43: Talking to My (Other) Self

Connections to research: As mentioned in Activity 42, when we commit to teaching, we may turn our backs on other career choices previously entertained. But we can still keep in touch with those old dreams.

Materials

None

Procedure

1. Think of an occupation that you have always been intrigued by or interested in, perhaps your dream job (e.g. artist, singer, athlete, lawyer, vet). It might be a job that you thought seriously of doing at one time but decided against. Maybe it's a career you always wonder if you *should* have chosen.

2. Have an imaginary conversation with this other self of yours. If it helps, sit opposite an empty chair and talk to the imaginary person sitting on it. Alternatively, you could write out an imaginary dialogue between your teacher self and that other self of yours. See the example below.

3. What surprised you in this imaginary conversation? What did you learn about yourself?

Example of an imaginary dialogue:

My teacher self (TS):	So, remind me, why did you ever want to be a vet, Tessa?
My vet self (VS):	I loved animals. I loved being on the farm. I wanted to work with horses and cows and to be outside a lot.
TS:	And what put you off, initially?
VS:	My teachers told me that women only got to treat budgies and kittens cos we're not strong enough for bigger animals. Also, I didn't realise that I was taking the wrong school subjects to get into vet school.
TS:	But, in my imagination, you did it anyway! What was vet school like?
VS:	A long, hard training and I was the only woman in the group! How was your training to be an English teacher?
TS:	It was great! Really sociable, met lots of foreigners, loved it! How were your first two years in the job as a vet?
VS:	Really hard! Lots of travelling in rural areas, trying to learn about so many kinds of cases, struggling to get farmers to trust me even though I was a just a skinny woman, out in all weathers, being kicked by cows!
TS:	How about the next few years?

VS:	There were terrible times, the Foot and Mouth outbreak, Mad Cow disease. I seemed to spend my working days dispatching sheep and putting cows down. Not what I had wanted to do with my career!
TS:	Did you manage to work with horses, as you'd wanted?
VS:	Yes, that is the one good thing. Although, I must say, I despair of many owners and their stupidity, causing their animals to get colic and laminitis, all sorts of preventable illnesses. How about you? Have you enjoyed your work?
TS:	In the main, I have absolutely loved it. Language education is a supportive, creative field and I have had many opportunities to travel, to learn, to write, and to experiment in classes. It's been great.
VS:	Sounds like you made a good decision to be a language teacher. What do you plan to do with your retirement?
TS:	I'd like to get some animals, a horse, a puppy, some hens, maybe a rabbit or two. We have a little bit of land so I fancy making a kind of small holding. What about you?
VS:	I thought I'd travel a bit and take up some foreign languages, maybe Italian or French! Maybe live abroad for a while.
TS:	Sounds like, in retirement, we might trade places!

Activity 44: Mapping the Future

Connections to research: Huberman encouraged teachers in his study to look back over their years of teaching. Having done this, however, it can help to look forward, too—not to try to predict the future but at least to consider what might be possible for you.

Materials

A large piece of paper and some coloured pens

Procedure

1. Get yourself into a musing frame of mind in your usual way, perhaps by going for a walk or playing music, thinking about a holiday, or poring over a map. Or consider the Lewis Carroll quote at the start of this section. We all need a little 'Wonderland' at times.

2. Start your musing! Perhaps consider some blue sky possibilities. Of course, what is blue sky for one person is grey to another, but imagine that . . . you are asked to take over your department, or you are offered the chance to go part time, or, the testing department needs a new staff member, or your painting hobby takes off and you start selling your work big time. Imagine that, like Alice, you 'walk' for a while. What areas of work would you like to pass through? What sort of places would you like to visit, professionally?

3. Using a large piece of paper and some coloured pens, flesh out your musings by creating a Wonderland map of your own to represent your professional future. It can have hills, valleys, mountains, rivers, bridges, all marked in whatever way you like. You could make it like a normal map with close contour lines for hills and mountains, red lines for major roads, blue lines for rivers, little outline trees for woods and forests, squares and rectangles for buildings, and so on.

   If you want things to stay roughly as they are in your work life, you might draw a large plateau, marked on your map with flowers to represent happy students and a sheltering tree to represent a benevolent, helpful boss. If you are ready for some real change, you might mark this with an abrupt change in the main road direction and a sign post. If you see difficult times ahead, you might draw a big river and add a bridge for the resources you will find to overcome the raging torrent!

From Implications to Application

Extensions and Variations

To delve further into teachers' feelings about work, Lewin Jones (2017) uses 12 road sign symbols to denote a dead end, a one-way street, a slippery road, zig zag bends, a roundabout, a motorway ahead, a steep slope upwards, uneven camber, a sharp right bend, a stop sign, danger of falling rocks, and the danger of a harbour wall.

You could incorporate these symbols into your map to express your feelings about your work future.

Further Reading

Lewin Jones, J. (2017). Signs of motivation: Using a visual stimulus for emotion-focused discussion in teacher training. *The Teacher Trainer*, *31*(1), 24–25.

Activity 45: From Known to New

Connections to research: This activity starts out the same as *How Do I Grow a Teaching Skill?* (Activity 13) but ends differently. It is for teachers who find themselves in a situation that is different from previous teaching because the content is new, the students are new and/or the context is new. We thus become like novices with respect to the new elements. However, one implication drawn from Tsui is the importance of understanding our history as teachers in order to be able to use our experience in new situations; thus, although we may feel like a novice again, we have a lot of experience to draw on that can help us navigate the new terrain.

Materials

A chart like this:

Things that were emphasised in my initial teacher-training	What I have learned about that skill so far	How I might apply this skill to **a new** situation

152

Procedure

1. Create a three-column chart as depicted in Materials, above.

2. In the left hand column, list things that you remember as being emphasised when you were in your initial training. Examples here could be: how to plan lessons, using your voice, posture and move-ment, organising the room, furniture and students, using a text book, making visual aids, correcting errors, and so on.

3. Taking one skill at a time, consider what you have learned about that skill so far and note this in the middle column.

4. Then choose the ones that you think will be most useful in your new situation and, in the right hand column, describe how you might use or adapt them.

Activity 46: An Eddy in the River

Connections to research: Huberman quotes many lively expressions used by teachers in his study to describe how they feel about their relationship to their institutions. This activity encourages this spirit of inventiveness.

Materials

An image of an eddy in a river

Procedure/Steps

1. Find an image of an eddy in a river or stream—an image that speaks to you.

2. Look at it carefully, considering it a metaphor for your professional situation.

3. Then ask yourself some interesting questions, such as:

In my professional life, what does the water in the river represent?

(The passage of time? The students coming through my classes?)

What are my river banks, my parameters at work?

(The room I work in? The curriculum? The rules of the institution?)

Do I feel the current is swift or slow? What eddy am I in? What is the holding pattern I am in right now? Are there any boulders or driftwood in my work and if so, what are they?

What would happen if the banks meta-phorically collapsed or a tree fell in? What sorts of things would these changes represent at work? How would I manage if they did?

Doing this work may help us to see our work situation more clearly and so protect ourselves against the challenges of change or lack of change.

Extensions and Variations

Poems, sayings, music, mime, dance, and drama can all be used as metaphors for our life and work. Allowing ourselves the freedom to use them as stimuli can uncover and reveal useful insights.

Activity 47: Graphic Organiser for Teacher Training and Development

Connections to research: Lortie's study identified a number of themes that have an impact on how teachers learn throughout their careers. There are many dynamics that underlie this learning.

Materials

None

Procedure

1. Make a list of the ideas that you associate with teacher training (e.g. *It's normally led by a trainer, has a curriculum made by others, leads to a qualification, is done with others, costs money, you often have to travel to do it,* etc.).

2. Make a list of the ideas that you associate with teacher development (e.g. *You can do it alone, off school premises, you state your own goals, it is not certified,* etc.).

3. Then consider the things that both concepts have in common (e.g. *both can lead to professional learning*).

4. Think about what sort of diagram or graphic organiser most closely represents your view of the relationship (or lack of relationship) between the two concepts. Are they polar opposites, in your view, thus belonging in separate boxes? Or do they belong on a scale so they can slide into one another? Would a yin yang symbol work better?

Extensions and Variations

Take any two other concepts that are important to you at work. Make notes on their features and then consider how you can diagram them to best advantage. Using a graph? A mind map? Intersecting clines? Spirals?

Further Reading

Freeman, D. (2016). *Educating second language teachers: The same things done differently*. Oxford: Oxford University Press.
Woodward, T. (1991). *Models and metaphors in the foreign language classroom*. Cambridge: Cambridge University Press.

Activity 48: I Plan, You Teach. You Plan, I Teach.

Connections to research: This activity connects to many of the points in Tsui's analysis of expertise: how our teaching reflects different points in our history, how we integrate different kinds of knowledge in our teaching, the importance of reflection and experimentation, and being open to learning from others.

Note

This activity works best when done by colleagues of very different lengths of teaching experience.

Materials

None

Procedure

1. Talk to a colleague about the classes you both teach. If you share a class, so much the better.

2. The more experienced teacher then writes a lesson plan for the less experienced to teach.

3. The less experienced teacher then uses the plan to teach a lesson with their own class.

4. After the taught lesson, the two teachers discuss how it went. Did the person who taught learn any new teaching moves as a result of the plan? Or do things in a different order or in a different way than usual?

5. Next, the less experienced teacher plans a lesson for the more experienced to teach.

6. The more experienced teacher then uses the plan to teach a lesson with their own class.

7. After this second taught lesson, the two teachers discuss how it went. The experienced teacher may have made changes to the plan or smoothed the plan in some way or may have been delighted to discover a freshness in terms of materials or approach.

Extensions and Variations

If you team up with a colleague of differing experience to yourself, there are all sorts of activities you can do together, such as:

- Observe some teaching (real or virtual) and discuss what stands out for each teacher. What do you each see?

- Write a case study together on, for example, spotting a discipline problem and dealing with it. Then discuss it together or with the rest of the staff.

- Offer to stay 30 minutes after school once a week to give out quick lesson plan ideas for less experienced staff for tomorrow's lessons.

- Divide up some reading. The less experienced teacher looks through some practical teaching magazines to find an activity they like, tries it out with a class and then teaches it to their colleague. The more experienced colleague trawls through research reports and high-lights useful Applied Linguistics studies and then summarises them for their colleague, perhaps mediating them in the ways suggested in Ur (2016).

- You can also form a school based Critical Friends Group (CFG) of seven or so teachers to meet monthly to examine students' work and teacher practices using protocols to guide the conversations. See Appendix.

Further Reading

Garcia-Stone, A. (2017). Professional development late in a teaching career. Part two. *The Teacher Trainer*, *31*(1), 17–19.

Ur, P. (2016). Why do language teachers need the research? *The Teacher Trainer*, *30*(1), 3–5.

From Implications to Application

Woodward, T. (2015). Professional development late in a teaching career. *The Teacher Trainer, 29*(3), 2–3.

Activity 49: Finding Balance Then Staying Interested

Connections to research: According to Huberman, after surviving the first few years of teaching, having found some satisfying routines to work with, there may come a time of stabilisation and then, later, we may need to keep learning to avoid feeling 'the stale breath of routine'.

Materials

The grid of possible Continuing Professional Development (CPD) activities (appears after 'Extensions and Variations' section for this activity)

Procedure

1. Look at the list of possible Continuing Professional Development (CPD) activities at the end of this activity.

2. Choose something from the left hand column of the list of CPD activities below that you are interested in (perhaps the idea of writing a blog or journal from section 7 of the list).

3. Think how you can do it. For example, if you chose writing a blog or journal, towards the end of a week's teaching, consider what events in the week have stuck in your mind.

   The events could be ones that amused, puzzled, pleased, or irritated you.

   You could jot down a few notes on these, taking care to record who the events involved, where and when they took place, what happened (zooming in on the close detail), and what the wider context was (zooming out).

It's a good idea to keep these notes together in a folder or notebook.

4. After a few weeks, look back on what you have got, reread and see if you can see any patterns emerging and then consider why the events happened and why they stuck in your mind.

    Maybe you have chosen, in addition or instead, the idea (from Section 1 of the grid of CPD activities) of having a structured subject discussion with colleagues.

    Your first topic could be 'Continuing Professional Development (CPD)' and the list itself could be useful to get things started.

    You could ask around to see who's interested and arrange for a CPD meeting with your fellow teachers in which you go through the list together.

    You could then pool your ideas on which organisations to join, what events to go to, or what topics to discuss. ('Critical Incidents in Teaching' could be one topic.) Or you could consider how to go about putting in a proposal for a conference.

Extensions and Variations

Since the original chart was put together in 2004, wonderful things have been happening for teachers online, so the chart has been updated accordingly. We now have online conferences and forum discussions, webinars and very useful teacher web sites. This means that, if we can't spare the money, time, or energy to go to conferences, on courses or away days, we can still learn extremely interesting things without stirring from our computers. Combining this learning with a 'study buddy' or in-house, professional development discussion with colleagues can be a very productive way of working.

CPD CHART[1]		
1. Associations, meetings, committees		
CPD Activity	**Do I do this?**	**My thoughts /actions**
Attend meetings of a professional association face to face or virtually		
Have structured subject discussions with colleagues		
Participate in staff development meetings/quality circles		
Do interviews with others in my job		

2. Conferences, seminars, webinars, fairs, courses		
CPD Activity	**Do I do this?**	**My thoughts/actions**
Produce and deliver a professional presentation, lecture, or webinar where this is not part of normal work duties		
Attend a seminar, webinar, workshop or conference		
Organise formal professional events		
Attend a course, online or face to face, or do self-study leading/not leading to examination or assessment		

3. Publications, materials, articles, papers		
CPD Activity	Do I do this?	My thoughts/actions
Write or evaluate in- or ex-house articles, text books, computer pro-grammes, learning materi-als, websites, etc.		
Review and pilot materials for a publisher		
Write a discussion paper or report for my department		

4. Consultancy, advising		
CPD Activity	Do I do this?	My thoughts/actions
Do consultancy work for the first time		

5. Job enrichment		
CPD Activity	Do I do this?	My thoughts/actions
Work shadow (follow and watch and learn to gain expertise)		
Try a job enrichment scheme (with expanded responsibilities/tasks/ roles, etc.)		
Visit another school or institution to find out about a successful innovation		
Share jobs		

6. Observation, mentoring		
CPD Activity	Do I do this?	My thoughts/actions
Be observed or tutored by peers, be a mentee		
Observe or peer tutor, be a mentor		
Team teach/team work		
Be observed by a line manager		
Observe yourself		

7. Professional inquiry projects		
CPD Activity	Do I do this?	My thoughts/actions
Try action research, class-room-based, or office-based exploratory teaching projects		
Write a job log, blog, or journal		
Analyse sections of student journals		
Write and discuss case studies or critical incidents		

Activity 50: Breaking Rules

Connections to research: According to Huberman, after surviving the first few years of teaching, having found some satisfying routines to work with, there may come a time of stabilisation and then, later, we may need to keep learning to avoid feeling stale. How can we break out of our own, once useful but now rather boring, routines?

Materials

None

Procedure

1. Brainstorm a list of basic ground rules that you abide by in your teaching. Examples might be:

    I write the day, time, and room number on my lesson plan to make sure I turn up in the right place at the right time

    I get into the classroom before the students arrive

    I greet the students in English

    I never leave the door open during a lesson

    I take the register at the start

    I never leave the room during the lesson

    I don't move furniture

    Students must put their hands up before they speak

    I always put my books and materials to the left of my desk as I face the class

    I always carry spare board pens with me in my bag

    I write IN CAPITALS on the board

> *I do not allow electronic dictionaries in class*
>
> *I set written homework every day*
>
> *Music is only for Fridays*
>
> . . .

If you brainstorm with a colleague, you will probably laugh at each other's guidelines. Your colleague's chewing gum rule and your own rule about students cracking their knuckles may make each other chortle!

2. The rules or guidelines that you come up with may have become habits for very good reasons. Perhaps they make you feel more secure and comfortable in class. Perhaps they are agreed school protocol. Perhaps colleagues have pressured you into NOT moving your furniture around as they don't like the noise. Some routines may have been ingrained in you through your time of being a student or perhaps during your teacher training. If you are happy with a rule, let it be. But if you feel that interesting things might happen if you broke one or two of your rules, then put an asterisk by them.

3. In this way, you are starting to notice your normal practice. Next, choosing a relatively unthreatening habit, choose to do the opposite of what you normally do. So, if you always ask students to underline the words in a text that they don't know, ask them to cirtcle them instead. Or ask them to tick all the nouns that they DO know instead. If you always call the register at the start of class, do it at the end of the lesson. Or ask a student to do it for you. Or ask students who finish a task early to do it together.

4. If you have colleagues you can talk to, share your rule breaking experiments with others. Or make a note of any changes you have tried and any interesting results.

5. Keep thinking about your routines, adding new areas such as student grouping, lesson stages, staff meetings, report writing, homework correction, or any other part of your working life that occurs to you. Try to figure out why you do things the way you normally do them. If the reason no longer holds good, or if you can't even remember the reason, make a change—break your own rules.

Further Reading

Fanselow, J. (1987). *Breaking rules: Generating and exploring alternatives in language teaching*. New York: Pearson. Also available, (2012). CreateSpace Independent Publishing Platform.

Activity 51: Moving On: Collecting or Throwing Away?

Connections to research: In a sense, this activity is in response to the public perception of teaching expressed by Lortie's concept of the 'one-step career'. This and the following activity examine how that time in teaching looks as we step out of it.

Materials

None

Procedure

1. If this is your last year or two of teaching before you retire, you may decide to prepare for the end of your current chapter of working life by collecting the kinds of things you think you will enjoy looking at later on (e.g. learner texts, thank you cards).

2. You may decide to search for patterns in the kinds of reports you have written or received over the years or to do *My Career Graph* (Activity 2) so you can look back over your professional life and get an overview of it.

3. Alternatively, you may decide to gradually throw away or give away the accumulations of notes, stationery, lesson plans, materials, and such that you have amassed over the years.

Activity 52: Moving On, Heading Out

Connections to research: In a sense, the ideas in the following activity are in response to the public perception of teaching expressed by Lortie's concept of the 'one-step career'. They examine how that time in teaching looks to us as we step out of it and help us to prepare for a massive change in our lives.

Materials

None

Procedure

If this is your last year or two of teaching before you retire, you may decide to prepare for the end of your current chapter of working life quite consciously so that you can arrange your feelings and leave with a sense of fulfillment and serenity. Ideas follow for smoothing the transition from work to retirement.

1. Shedding:

   a. Cut down on your schedule, if it is possible in your situation, so that you teach fewer hours per day or per week. This will help you to figure out what you want to do once you have more choices in a day.

   b. Start shedding any extra roles and responsibilities, too, that you have gathered outside your main role (e.g. resource centre librarian, induction mentor, in service trainer, exams co-ordinator, staff representative). Put your energy into ensuring the sustainability of these roles and into a positive handover.

c. Go through your notes, stationary, lesson plans, and other materials, and think about any you would want to keep as a mentor. Consider which of your colleagues (perhaps new teachers, early or mid-career teachers, the school librarian, or teacher educator/ trainer colleagues) might welcome receiving these materials.

2. Collecting:

Start collecting the kinds of things you think you will enjoy looking at later on when you are no longer teaching (e.g. learner texts, thank you cards, photos of yourself with happy groups, leaving presents from students).

3. Analysing:

a. Search for patterns in the kinds of reports you have written or received over the years.

b. Do *My Career Graph* (Activity 2) at the beginning of Section B so you can look back over your professional life and get an overview of it.

c. Consider what the high points of your teaching life have been.

d. Consider what you could leave behind you when you go, either for fun (e.g. a jargon generator made from topical buzz words) or for some kind of professional legacy (e.g. a file of warm up activities colleagues can use).

e. Organise a 'Talking Shop' gathering, as in *Talking Shop* (Activity 7).

In Section D we have encouraged you to consider where the edges of your competence lie and how you can push on in your development. You have had the opportunity to consider who you might become, how

From Implications to Application

colleagues can help you to grow, ways you can use what you know in new situations, how to intentionally upset your own status quo, and how you can map your own future. In short, to look ahead and think, 'What's next?'

Note

1 These charts are adapted from Woodward, T. (2004) *Ways of working with teachers*. Elmstone; TW Pubs. pp. 204–206, courtesy of Fiona Balloch who wrote the original list for BIELT.

Part 3

From Application to Implementation

In Part 3 we describe ways that teachers can organise and use the activities in Part 2 either on their own or with colleagues both near and far. We also look at ways the activities can be used as part of the Continuing Professional Development (CPD) programme within an institution, as well as ways that teacher educators can use the activities with teachers on teacher development courses. A comprehensive use of the activities in Part 2 would take in our three main questions, 'Where have I/we come from?' 'Where am I/are we now?' 'Where do I/we want to go?' So these three questions and the activities related to them could be used as an overall pathway in any circumstance. However, we discuss other pathways below.

A. If You Are a Teacher Who Prefers Working on Your Own

We'll start with a teacher interested in using the ideas and activities in this book on their own, either through choice or circumstance. A teacher who, like the authors, has spent many years as a student in classrooms in primary, secondary, and tertiary level education, can find it interesting to look back on all that schooling to consider how one's awareness of teaching, learning, and classrooms has changed over time.

When one of the authors (that's me, Tessa) was a pupil at secondary school, I did realise that teachers sometimes changed their ideas about how to do their work. I knew this because our French teacher, Miss Martin, came in one Monday and told us that we were going to use as much French as possible in each lesson from then on, so that French would become the language of the class and not just something we studied in a lesson by talking about it in English. She said we were going to aim to get 80% of all talk in her lessons in French! We started right there and then by learning how to answer her new greeting, 'Bonjour la classe!' with 'Bonjour Madame!' It was quite a shake-up.

I also realised that the new, young teachers joining the secondary school staff did different kinds of activities and used different materials from the older teachers. They did pair work and used role play cards, for example. So I knew teachers differed from each other and also that, individually, they changed their modus operandi from time to time. I connected this variation to a few individual personalities on the staff rather than realising that many of our teachers might be thinking and working out how to hone their skills bit by bit over a teaching career. I certainly was not conscious of how much I was myself absorbing about teaching and learning from my own time of being in classes as a student. I didn't think, even when I started out myself in my first teaching job, in terms of gradual development over a career. In fact, looking back now, I wish I had known that teaching English actually *was* a real career rather than a relatively short term job, and also a career with different pathways, stages, and phases—one where the learning can go on and on socially, psychologically, pedagogically, cognitively, and linguistically, even when, perhaps especially when, you are working and developing on your own. You, gentle reader, holding this book in your hand, may well be more aware of all these things than I ever was.

We teachers live full, busy lives, both in and outside of the schools or institutions in which we work. The aim of professional development is for it to be doable, rewarding, sustainable and to give us work satisfaction and aid the learning of our students. This means considering how to incorporate it into our teaching lives in feasible ways, doing enough to gain satisfaction and momentum, but not so much as to be overwhelmed and give up before we can reap its benefits. In the long run, gradually working on our own skills and our own enthusiasms and puzzles may be the most sustainable of all types of professional development because, as an individual teacher, we alone are the ones who decide when we have the time and energy to do it. We are the ones who know how we learn best. We have complete control over what we do and when we do it. And we can choose any hook we like to pique our interest and get us started. Some such hooks follow!

Ways to Proceed

If You Like Reading . . .

Choose a passage about research from this book, perhaps one of the passages in Part 1 relating to the researchers mentioned, or indeed a passage from one of the research-based leads cited so far in the book. Set aside some time to read and think. Make a set of symbols for yourself that you can use to code your reactions to different parts of the passage you have chosen to read. Here are some suggestions:

√ = I agree
X = I disagree
? = I don't think I understand this
! = That surprises me

Then, as you read, stop every so often and consider how you feel about what you have just read. As well as doing your usual highlighting or note taking, use your code to record on the text your reactions to each part. It's a good idea to keep a reading log, too, where you write down the title and author of the passage, the date you read it, and any quotations or learning points you want to remember from it. You might want to try *Letter to a Mentor* (Activity 21) as a way of further exploring what you learn from the reading.

If you have chosen to start with passages from Part 1 of this book, you might like to go on to review the beginning of Part 2, which summarises the implications of the research discussed in Part 1 and cross references it with the activities that follow in Part 2. Consider implications from the research that you are interested in exploring and choose relevant activities to do.

If You Like Thinking About the Past . . .

Do the second activity in Part 2 entitled *My Career Graph* (Activity 2) and spend time mulling over how things have gone for you, career wise, so far and the phases and themes you have experienced. These phases and themes may suggest particular areas you want to pursue by reading, thinking, or experimenting. Other activities that can trigger this kind of work are *Material Changes* (Activity 4) and *Methodological Changes* (Activity 5).

If You Like 'To Do' Lists . . .

Many people like writing lists, crossing off items that they have already done, rewriting undone things onto later lists, rewriting lists in priority order, and so on! If you get organised in this way too, you might like to try the activity *Finding Balance Then Staying Interested* (Activity 49), which has a long enough list to keep anybody going for years, or the activity *Where Do I Want to Go Next?* (Activity 37).

If You Like Being Creative . . .

You can use your memory, your imagination, new thinking frameworks, role play, and metaphor to explore your CPD in the following activities from Part 2: *Ghosts Behind the Blackboard* (Activity 6), *They Keep Getting Younger!* (Activity 25), *How Can I Respond Creatively to a Difficult Stage of My Professional Life Cycle?* (Activity 19), *Who I Could Become* (Activity 42), *Half-Scripted Interviews* (Activity 34), *Talking to My (Other) Self* (Activity 43), and *A 'Good' Teacher Is . . .* (Activity 38).

If You Are Going Through a Tricky Patch . . .

By doing the activity *Facing a Difficult Stage in My Professional Life Cycle* (Activity 18) you can start to figure out what the problem is and then consider how to begin to tackle it. You may want to continue by doing activities such as *Critical Incidents* (Activity 9), *Building Case Studies* (Activity 28), *Freirean Problem Posing* (Activity 29), and *An Eddy in the River* (Activity 46), following up each time with entries in a self-reflection notebook. If the tricky patch is related to feeling like a novice again, either because you are in a new place, are teaching new content, or are working with a different kind of student, *What's in My Teaching Suitcase?* (Activity 40) and *From Known to New* (Activity 45) may help you regain confidence.

If You Like Experimenting . . .

Huberman points out that teachers who experiment in different ways in their practice may, later on in their careers, feel more satisfied with their teaching lives. Tsui goes even further to say that when teachers engage in experimentation, they renew and widen their existing knowledge about teaching. They draw on both practical knowledge from their own experience as well as knowledge from research that helps them to understand and improve their practice. So there are good reasons for choosing this particular way of continuing your professional development. Activities that can be useful here are: *Transformative Times* (Activity 11), *How Do I Grow a Teaching Skill?* (Activity 13), *How Do I Grow a Teacher Learning Technique?* (Activity 39), *Breaking Rules* (Activity 50), *How Can I Check My Pedagogical Competence?* (Activity 20), and *Constraints and Resources of My Teaching Context* (Activity 32).

If You Like Learning From Students . . .

We were all language students once and many of us still are. The activity *Language Learning Autobiography* (Activity 10) can help us to reveal and concretise what we have already absorbed about life in the language classroom from our time behind the desk!

When it comes to our own students, we can learn a lot from them too. Activities you might like to try out to do this are: *A Course Book Page We Love/Hate* (Activity 24), *They Keep Getting Younger!* (Activity 25), *Dialogue Journals* (Activity 27), and *How Do I See My Students?* (Activity 26).

If You Like to Have a Concrete Aim . . .

After you have tried out some of the activities mentioned above, you might like to think of a target to reach to keep you motivated. For example, you might decide to blog about your reading, thinking, or experimentation. *Writing An Op-Ed* (Activity 35) gives suggestions for how to write an opinion piece about something you care about.

From Application to Implementation

You could write an article for your local teachers' newsletter or for an international ELT periodical, such as the ones below:

- *English Australia Journal*: www.englishaustralia.com.au/journal

- *ELT Journal:* www.oxfordjournals.org/our_journals/eltj/about.html

- *English Teaching Forum*: http://exchanges.state.gov/forum/

- *The Essential Teacher*: www.tesol.org/s_tesol/seccss. asp?CID=206&DID=1676

- *Modern English Teacher*: www.onlinemet.com/

- TESL online journal: http://tesl-ej.org/ej46/toc.html

- *English Teaching Professional*: www.etpmagazine.com/

- *Humanising Language Teaching magazine*, an online periodical: www.HLTmag.co.uk

- *The Teacher Trainer: www.tttjournal.co.uk*

Alternatively, you might decide to go on a teacher training course to upgrade your qualifications. Or you could plan to read a certain number of ELT articles a month, or to listen to a certain number of the 30 or so interviews with teachers carried out by Darren Elliott and archived on his YouTube channel: www.youtube.com/ playlist?list=PLc0c80JO4j4Ez1advZxQdZzDBkaHmot6x

If You Have Access to the Internet . . .

The British Council's Teaching for Success programme has developed a CPD framework for teachers and teacher trainers which helps you to assess your own skills and knowledge and to identify the PD you need to develop further in key areas of teaching. To get started, visit the 'Continuing professional development' page at www.teachingenglish. org.uk/teacher-development

B. If You Are a Teacher Who Prefers to Work Face to Face With a Couple of Colleagues

Lortie used the term 'egg-crate' profession to describe the way in which teachers are isolated, with each of us cocooned in our own private classroom. The positive side of this is the autonomy we have because, once 'the door is closed', we can teach pretty much how we like. The negative side is our separation from colleagues, which inhibits collegiality and learning from each other. We all know how stimulating it can be to explain what we are trying out or what we are grappling with or to hear from another teacher about what he or she is working on. It is even more rewarding when we can get together purposefully to spend time learning together—with and from each other. We can find out about others and share issues among teachers with the same or similar types of classes, the same lengths of experience, or we can band together across different types of classes and lengths of experience.

Ways to Proceed

Getting Started

You may have a colleague or two that you love to work with, whether by staying after class to plan lessons together, or feeling able to moan and groan to each other when things go awry, or even by managing a spot of turn teaching, where one teacher animates the class while the other is back stage or team teaching where both teachers are working to animate the class, possibly by doing a dialogue in front of the class or supporting different groups in their work. When time permits, see if your colleagues would like to do a bit more professional development with you. Have an initial discussion, perhaps reminding each other of how you got into the profession, what you feel about the work, what you'd like to keep the same and to change in your work. Discuss the sorts of activities that you could do together (see below) and keep it realistic as to who is expected to do what by when. It's usually better to start slowly and be able to sustain momentum rather than to burn yourselves out in a flurry of over-ambitious, initial enthusiasm!

Using the Activities in This Book

Every one of the activities in Part 2 can be done with one or more colleagues. Doing the activities together is a mutually enriching experience helping us to devise creative responses to the particular stage of our professional lives we are in or the theme we are experiencing at a particular time. You could try out the activities *I Plan, You Teach. You Plan, I Teach* (Activity 48), *Checking Bad Habits!* (Activity 14) and *Who Is My 'Go To Person'?* (Activity 41). You could also try *Moving On, Heading Out* (Activity 52) if you are at differing levels of experience.

Doing Some Reading

Having chosen an article from a practical teaching magazine, either the same one for you and your colleagues, or different ones for different people, read the article in your own time. You can annotate it as you read using the code mentioned in the 'If You Like Reading . . .' section just above, but add a new symbol such as a hash tag # or an asterisk * to denote an idea or activity that you would like to try out in your own classes. Try it out when you have an opportunity. Then, when you get together to discuss the article with your colleagues, you can use the symbols to structure your discussion and can also report back on the new idea you tried out. If you have chosen the same activity to try out, that also stimulates good discussion as to how it works with or can be adapted for different levels or types of class.

Talking About Shared Classes

If you share a class or classes with the colleagues that you are joining up with, it makes sense to use that common ground as a basis for professional development. Some conversations between different teachers of the same class can, however, be rather unhelpful. We're sure you know the sort of thing we mean.

Here's an example.

Teacher A: I am very worried about class/student X. They seem very distracted and unruly.

Teacher B: Oh, I don't know what you mean. They are absolutely angelic with me!

Here's another one.

Teacher A: I did a new activity with them today. It worked really well! It's called an X activity.

Teacher B: Oh, that old X activity. I've been doing that for years! Very old hat.

And another:

Teacher A: Something interesting happened in class today. X said, 'Y' and then Z just walked out!

Teacher B: Oh, yeah? That reminds me. The other day there was this guy and . . . (hijacks the topic for the next 5 minutes)

And the last one, we promise!

Teacher A: Did you take your class out into the garden? or Did you show them a video today instead of on Friday afternoon? I thought we weren't supposed to do that.

Teacher B: . . . (Bitter silence!)

These are examples of the kinds of exchanges where nobody really learns anything. One teacher might get to feel a bit superior, the other inferior. But we can't really see these teachers professionally developing over time together! And yet we all fall prey to these conversational dead ends. It takes discipline to avoid them! One way to improve things is to talk about these kinds of exchanges, ones such as those above, ones that drive you and the colleagues you are working with mad. You can give them nicknames such as 'Angelic' and 'Old hat'. Then, when you start discussing your shared classes, you can alert each other, with humour and good will, to the conversational traps you are falling into. Point them out by saying, for example,

'Oh, I think we just did a 'Not supposed to' Ooops!'

Apart from avoiding annoying conversational road blocks, we can make conversations about shared classes more productive by initially choosing an unthreatening focus. Here are some possible topics to start off with:

- Where do you do your lesson planning?

- What is the very first/last thing you do in that class as you walk in/out?

- Do you set homework? What sort? How do you mark it?

- How do you check attendance?

Once you have built trust between you, other topics might be:

- Which student do you feel you know best and least? Why?

- Between us two different teachers, do we think we are giving the students a good course? Are we missing anything out? Are we duplicating anything?

- What do the students get from you that I can't give them so easily and vice versa?

If you and your colleagues feel your way, discussing carefully which topics and which conversational gambits are constructive and which not, you are likely to have some very useful professional exchanges.

Observing and Discussing Teaching

In a busy school, it may be too difficult for you to arrange cover of your own class so that you can watch another teacher at work in class or so that they may watch you. So, if you want to do some observation and discussion of an observed class with your colleagues, you may need to go online and find a video. The advantage of this is that you can watch it in your own time, where you like. But whether you watch a real class or a recorded one, you will want to avoid the discussion afterwards becoming overly critical of the poor teacher at work! A very useful question to ask, as an observer of any class being taught by someone else, is:

What can I learn about *my own* teaching from watching this person at work?

Sharing the answers to this question with a colleague can be very fruitful and takes away the praise and blame of another (distant) colleague.

Preparing a Presentation Together

Working with a colleague or colleagues as study buddies on a professional presentation for an in-house teacher development session can be a great way to learn, whether your presentation is theoretical, practical, or a mixture of both. Theory can be vague, so preparing a presentation together may force you to reread theoretical ideas to clarify and to consider practical implications that make sense in your setting.

Keeping Track of How It's Going

Whatever hook you choose to get you started and to keep you motivated, however consistent or sporadic your own personal CPD programme is, and whether or not you have a friend or two to work with, it is a good idea to keep a journal of what you have done, when, and why, and what you feel you have learned. This way you can gain a feeling of progress as you look at the journal now and then over time. The activity *Yearly Retrospective* (Activity 8) can help here. A teacher learning journal or yearly retrospective log can help, too, if you are preparing for a job or course interview. It is proof of your personal investment in your own professional development.

C. If You Are a Teacher Interested in a CPD Programme in an Institution

Many, if not most, language teachers work in an institution of some kind, whether this is a primary or secondary school, an institute of tertiary education, a business school, a private language school, or a language department nestled within an army college or other specialist company. Even lone, freelance teachers often go into educational institutions such as business schools to do their teaching. And many of these establishments recognise that having a commitment to the professional development of their staff gives pay offs, such as attracting more qualified and professional staff, retaining staff by treating them as professionals, getting better results in terms of student learning and satisfaction, achieving higher ratings with inspection bodies, ensuring good inter-departmental relations, and increasing ability to respond to change. It may be that you have a particular interest or role in creating or influencing the professional development opportunities in the institution in which you work.

The overall ethos and life of an institution can support the continuing professional development of all staff, including management, teachers, support staff, office administrators, caretakers, and canteen workers in many practical ways. Initial meetings of staff to discuss these ways may come up with some of the following ideas for supporting professional development, as well as other ideas. The list below may also give food for thought about possibilities you might not have considered.

Ideas for Supporting Professional Development in an Institution

- Having a statement, contributed to by all staff, that describes the institution's commitment to Professional Development and that is visible on websites, noticeboards, and in staff files.

- Issuing clear job descriptions that are regularly reviewed by those who actually do the jobs.

- Running induction sessions for new staff.

- Providing on-the-job training as necessary when laws, policies, materials used, and other things change.

- Informing staff of health and safety, equal opportunity, and other issues.

- Conducting staff development interviews with all staff regularly.

- Encouraging membership in professional organisations.

- Encouraging attendance at and presentations by staff at F2F and virtual courses, seminars, conferences.

- Having a regular in house programme of PD events.

- Having a part-time PD representative for all staff sectors to support individuals in their professional interests, including publication.

- Encouraging teams and cross sector networks with clear routes of communication throughout the institution.

- Setting up a peer observation and/or job shadowing systems.

- Giving out information on short courses on job-related issues such as First Aid, safeguarding, and so on.

- Encouraging staff to gain qualifications.

- Encouraging regular discussions of political, economic, social, and educational changes the institution must respond or adapt to, in order to stay buoyant and current.

Thinking at a slightly more philosophical level, Huberman makes two suggestions of relevance here. One is that a 'life cycle orientation' could influence the way that a school administration works with or 'manages' teachers. This implies that one size of PD will NOT fit all! There will need to be 'different strokes for different folks' because staff will be in different phases of their careers and enjoying or suffering different personal themes in their work at any particular time.

Another suggestion from Huberman is that it could be of value to inscribe in the life of an educational institution some common havens for professional reflection around the themes in his study. These havens could be represented by comfortable discussion areas in a staffroom (plus free coffee and biscuits!), a shared high-tech social network, a private part of a web site, a CPD notice board, a regular slot in a F2F PD meeting, or other ways more fitting for the place where you work.

Our own suggestion in terms of setting an overall tone is that, whatever PD statement is made by an educational institution, whatever practical or philosophical means are used to discuss it and carry it out, staff must have a voice in what is planned and done, and not have things done to them or forced on them. This implies instituting regular ways to consult with teaching staff about their needs as well as ways to check back on PD implementation to find out whether their needs have been/are being met.

In the light of all the above, it may be useful to adapt the three questions in Part 2 of this book for discussion within an educational institution:

> Where have we come from in terms of PD in this institution?

> Where are we now in terms of PD in this institution?

> Where do we want to go from now on in terms of PD in this institution?

Ways to Proceed

Getting an Overview of Who Is on the Staff

Once the fundamental discussions have taken place to set the overall tone of CPD and to consider practical ways of expressing this tone, those responsible for co-ordinating the PD need to consider the best way to find out about the teachers on the staff. How many mentors and mentees are there? How many first-year teachers? How many fairly established, more experienced, and expert teachers are there?

Getting an Overview of Staff Learning

It is also wise to find out what people are *already* learning, whether from their classes, with colleagues, by individual reading, by attendance at outside evening classes, or from hobbies and courses. It is unrealistic and condescending to assume that teachers are blank slates awaiting enlightenment! Many will have their own learning projects on the go.

Analysing Overall Teacher Professional Development Needs

Then we need to consider how to find out what teachers want or need to learn next. To build a picture of learning at our institution we can use *Yearly Retrospective* (Activity 8), and also hold discussion at meetings chaired by different people in rotation on different occasions, by using questionnaires, by individual mini presentations or posters, via notice boards and staff newsletters, or by looking for patterns that come up in (peer) observation and discussion or from staff development interviews.

From this we can build a picture of what PD issues all the staff have in common. An example here might be 'The need for resilience' since this is an important aspect to consider whether you are struggling to survive at the start of your teaching career, trying to avoid burnout in the middle, or fighting to stay engaged at other points. (For a useful article on resilience, see Mansfield et al., 2016.) With such issues of common concern, the topic can be chosen and all staff of whatever level of experience given a month to read, peer observe, and reflect before meeting to discuss the topic from their different perspectives.

Responding to Sectional Needs

Other issues raised will be more sectional. For instance, novice teachers may be interested in gaining practical ideas so they can build routines (in, for example, greeting classes, marking phases of the lesson, working with texts, setting up pair and group work, setting useful homework, and so on). Changing routines will be more of a need for over-routinised teachers (see *Breaking Rules* (Activity 50), *How Do I Grow A Teaching Skill?* (Activity 13), and *Checking Bad Habits!* (Activity 14)). Disrupting

From Application to Implementation

the apprenticeship of observation to allow for the new may come up for other teachers. (*From Tactics to Beliefs* (Activity 31) may be helpful here.) Older staff may be puzzled by changes in student behaviour in class (see *They Keep Getting Younger!* (Activity 25)) or may be ready for a long hard look back over their careers (see *How Did I Become an English Language Teacher?* (Activity 1)). It may therefore make sense to work in smaller groups or in pairs of teachers with the same or similar levels of experience or to group together those sharing similar themes of interest and concern.

Gaining Individual Perspectives

Many issues will be of much more concern to one individual than to others. In this case, teachers can choose their own focus, try out an activity from Part 2 that appeals to them, and meet once a month to present and discuss their reflections with others. To respond well to these individual concerns, it is important, too, to create a PD system that allows for reverse mentoring. This idea from Huberman (p. 263) reverses the usual system of a mentor suggesting to a mentee what they could do to improve their teaching. Instead it is the mentee who makes the suggestions. It allows for an individual teacher to request, for example, a change of levels/grades of students at the end of some years of teaching, request periods of absence to retrain, or ask to have a reduction in load when, for example, dealing with a period of difficulty at home. Other teachers may ask for support to join in with a local network for professional exchange or experimentation.

Keeping Track of How It's Going

Just as it is important to involve everyone on the staff in setting the ethos of PD in an institution, in choosing practical ways to represent that tone, and in discussing a way to proceed, we also need to figure out a way to check what we are doing.

One suggestion here is to list the sorts of topics or themes used so far in PD sessions and to ask for feedback on these as well as for suggestions for new topics or themes. This can be done in a simple handout such as the one sketched below.

Feedback Form

Below are the variety of themes we have had at some PD meetings this term. Please mark after each one whether you want to retain them and how often you want them (*) or discontinue them (X). Please also feel free to note briefly your reasons why.

Apologies for absence

Menu for the meeting

Ideas swap

Top tips

Report back from conferences and courses

My favourite bad habit

What I've been working on lately

New materials in the resources room

Discussion of reading given out last time

New people/new roles

What's the marketing/accommodation/testing/curriculum department up to?

Back to basics (Remember? When we took photos of our boards before and after the input session on 'Using the Board')

Open flexi-spot

Free biscuits

Action points

And can you also make notes on the issues below please . . .?

Themes you would like to have in future

> *What (mini) sessions you can offer*
>
> *Is one hour about the right length?*
>
> *Is Monday afternoon the best time for a PD session?*
>
> *What has been particularly helpful and why?*
>
> *Thank you!*
>
> *Signed*
>
> *Your Professional Development Co-ordinator for this year*

Reviewing What Has Been Achieved

As well as checking often that PD meeting themes are useful and interesting to staff, you will want to keep track of the PD events and interests each year. One idea is to write an annual account of the PD that has been undertaken and to circulate this for comment so that staff have a reminder of sessions held, courses and conferences attended and by whom, articles accepted for publication, qualifications gained, and so on. This more formal document, together with the *Yearly Retrospective* (Activity 8), and any system of logging reflections from peer observations will help staff to see the institution as a place where lots of learning is happening on the staff side as well as in the language classes. It also means that participants develop a shared discourse that can strengthen the institution and bring coherence to working within it.

D. If You Are a Teacher Interested in Collaborating Across Local Institutions

Working alone, with a colleague or two face to face, or within a professional development programme at an institution are all good ways of learning, building skills, and staying interested in the job. Another possibility, and one Huberman notes in his study under the theme of 'activism', is the idea of setting up or joining a network of teachers, either at different institutions locally or by using social media and learning platforms of various types to create virtual groups.

This branching out may be a step too far for the debutante teacher busy planning lessons and learning basic routines. The settled teacher, too, may be more interested in experimenting within the classroom and within the institution they work in. But for some, the idea of going beyond the confines of our own teaching establishment is exciting and likely to keep us fresh in our careers for a bit longer!

Although the institutions in your area involved in the same or similar types of work may be business competitors, individual teachers within them can still find lots of ways of cooperating on CPD that do not directly impact on the financial bottom line. Work can be done between teachers on general local issues, such as how to attract more students into the area or how best to liaise with local police if, for example, incoming young adult students are facing hostility on the streets from local youths. Work can also be done on a targeted issue such as the implementation of new laws on safeguarding under-age students or the feasibility of setting up a regional exam centre for use by local schools with exam preparation classes.

The first actions are to note what institutions there are in your local area, to suggest that relevant people put out feelers to see if the institutions would be interested in some form of co-operation on teacher development, and then to instigate a few initial meetings to see whether co-operation is possible. If it is important to avoid a charge of 'empire building' by one dominant institution or of 'benign industrial espionage', offer a name for the network such as 'The X Region Round Table', suggest meeting in different schools and with different chairs each time, and keep the discussion off marketing or business topics.

In a local area, face-to-face encounters can be supplemented with email, Skype, other social media, Dropbox, or an Internet chatroom. Ideas from Part 1 and Part 2 of this book can be offered to get things going.

As well as larger meetings on topics like the ones above, consider the idea of teachers meeting in smaller numbers. Teachers who teach similar sorts of classes, who share similar passions or problems, and who have similar lengths of experience will enjoy meeting others locally to compare notes and swap ideas. However, teachers with differing lengths of experience may also like the idea of mentoring or of being mentored by a colleague from a different institution, someone who doesn't know the 'politics' of their own staff room!

E. If You Are a Teacher Trainer About to Run a Short Professional Development Course

As a teacher trainer or teacher educator, you may wish to offer a short intensive course on Professional Development for teachers in your area or from further afield or to run a part-time one over a longer time span. Though it is possible that some colleagues from the same institution will join the course together, the chances are that participants on such courses will have widely different training, work contexts, and experiences and not know each other. This can be an advantage as it increases the likelihood of interesting discussions among participants. A course such as this can also be a great opportunity for teachers to leave the confines of their own institution and the routines of their own staff rooms for longer than in the regional co-operation mentioned in the previous section, and to gain insights into their own careers and working practices from discussions with other professionals they do not know. The opportunity to exchange ideas with teachers is sometimes more important than the actual focus of the PD course itself.

Before the Course

You will want to contact participants before the course, if at all possible, not just to get as much information as you can about their context, length, and type of experience; teaching qualifications; and language proficiency, but also to encourage them to bring some things with them. Examples here are: an activity for the language class they are willing to demonstrate, a course book or set of materials they often work with, and one or two teaching issues they would like to discuss with others during the course. You might also ask them to bring something 'historical' to reflect how times have changed for them, such as a list of materials and activities they used to use but don't use any more, or an old course book they no longer have to use. Explain that the course will give them a chance to air their work concerns and puzzles, to exchange practical ideas using their 'bring with' resources with fellow participants, co-ordinated by an experienced tutor and in a collaborative atmosphere.

A Way to Proceed

If you would like an overall pathway for your course, whatever the length of experience of the participants you expect, you could divide the time up under the following questions or headings for consideration by participants:

Where have I come from professionally?

Where am I now in my work life?

Where would I like to go next?

This echoes the questions used by us to organise Part 2 of this book. These are answerable by any teacher no matter how many years of experience they have and also would mean that all the activities in Part 2 then become available for you to work with under a three-part structure.

Working With the First Question

You could work with the first question at the start of the course. Along with your usual methods of helping people to get to know each other's names and backgrounds, you could use some of the activities from Part 2 of this book—for example, *How Did I Become an English Teacher?* (Activity 1), *Describing My Work* (Activity 33), *Transformative Times* (Activity 11), and *Professional Development Survey* (Activity 12).

You will want to continue learning about your participants throughout your time together so you may like to consider using *Dialogue Journals*

From Application to Implementation

(Activity 27) or trying some other form of individual letter writing—that is, if you have enough time between sessions. It also depends on the number of participants who take you up on the offer of a private, written, one-to-one with the trainer. The idea can be adapted for use between participants and when carried out this way can serve as a good trial of the activity for those considering going on to use dialogue journals with their own language classes.

Working With the Second Question

If you choose to work with the second question, 'Where am I now?' in the next phase of the course, you could use the activities *My Career Graph* (Activity 2) or *Facing a Difficult Stage in My Professional Life Cycle* (Activity 18) from Part 2 to start things off.

It's a good idea to get into the ideas, materials, and issues that participants have brought with them as fast as possible, to make sure the course is maximally relevant and useful to them.

To work with the language learning activities that some participants may have brought with them, allow time for a participant to explain the activity to you first, to gather any necessary materials for it, and then plan a short slot of course time for them to demonstrate it, with their colleagues acting as language students.

To work with the course materials that participants have brought with them, you can adapt the activity *A Course Book Page We Love/Hate* (Activity 24). Provide everyone with a copy of the pages chosen by your first volunteer and give everyone time to peruse them. On a part-time course, this is no problem. On an intensive course, you will need to think a couple of days ahead. Next, ask the volunteer to present their most/least favourite section along with a little background and their reasons for finding the material winning or troublesome. After allowing for questions, brainstorm ideas for using the material in language classes with fellow PD course participants.

In order to work with the puzzles, issues, and teaching concerns that participants have brought with them, it is a good idea to give a homework task very early on in a short, intensive course, possibly on the first evening.

Ideas from Part 2, such as the activity *Building Case Studies* (Activity 28), *Critical Incidents* (Activity 9), *Freirean Problem Posing* (Activity 29), and *Teaching Bump* (Activity 30) can all be used to animate the concerns participants have brought with them. For example, if you choose to use *Building Case Studies*, you can ask people to write down their concern as a case study and hand it in to you so that you can gauge whether it is clear enough for others to understand and then discuss. If it isn't, write a few questions or comments on the text and suggest an expansion. If you prefer, you can prime the pump by offering an example of your own. This will need to be a real concern you have about your work and one you are prepared to have discussed openly. Alternatively, you can ask participants to read each other's first draft case study and to check if there is enough information contained in it to go on.

Case studies can be discussed one by one in the whole group. This will obviously take time and not all puzzles will be as riveting as others.

To deal with more case studies more quickly, and to cut down on the possibility that some issues may not be of great interest to absolutely all the other participants, the texts can be placed in numbered envelopes and sheets of blank paper made available or they can be posted online in a gated Internet environment. Individual participants, or pairs, can choose an envelope, or a numbered case online, note down the number, read the case study and, after reflection (and discussion, if working in a pair) can write their thoughts under the two questions:

How many problems do you see?

What possible solutions do you see?

The participants can write their comments and put them back in the envelope and back on the table for others to pick up or they can post their comments online. They then choose another case study with a different number and repeat the procedure. Run the activity until all the case studies have been read and commented on by at least two different people. Then the owners of the case studies take them back. Their job is, for homework, to read the comments and suggestions written by others on their case study, to summarise these, and present their thoughts to the group either orally, by poster, or online.

Working With the Third Question

To work with the third question, 'Where do I want to go next?' in the next phase of the course, any of the following activities from Part 2 of this book would be useful: *Where Do I Want to Go Next?* (Activity 37), *Mapping the Future* (Activity 44), *How Do I Grow a Teacher Learning Technique?* (Activity 39), *Who I Could Become* (Activity 42), *Finding Balance Then Staying Interested* (Activity 49), and *Talking to My (Other) Self* (Activity 43).

These activities could be supplemented by jigsaw reading tasks using texts on suitable topics for PD, and topics raised by participants such as peer observation, team teaching, and action research.

As well as these larger chunks of work, individual activities from Part 2 of this book can be used as warm up activities each day. This way, participants can continue to learn more about each other. An example here is *A 'Good' Teacher Is . . .* (Activity 38).

The main idea is not to stuff the course with activities, even if they are themed according to the three organising questions, but rather to choose a few that you feel would be interesting catalysts for reflection, writing, discussion, and sharing of ideas and then to allow plenty of time for this, working as much as possible with the participants' own content.

Tangible Products

It is a good idea to work towards a tangible product from the course.

Examples here might be:

- A journal of a participant's thoughts in answer to the three organising questions.

- A personal plan of future PD actions detailing what is to be done, by when, what steps will need to be taken, what resources needed, and so on.

- A scrapbook of practical ideas for use in their own language classes.

- A mind map of the main issues presented and discussed on the course (see *Graphic Organiser for Teacher Training and Development* (Activity 47) too).

- A write up of a case study plus ensuing discussion.

- An essay on what it is like to be behind a desk again after many years.

The last two could be offered for publication in a local, regional, national, or international teacher association newsletter or on a Teacher Development Special Interest Group (SIG) blog or website.

Follow Up

It is very important to provide leads to resources which participants can use after returning home and if and when they want to continue the impetus for professional development started on the course.

If you plan to introduce participants to resources on the Internet, then a thread on the course such as showing 'A website a day', backed up with an email message containing all the links used in the course, makes more sense than a list written on a handout and given out on the last day.

The prime resource for the participants will be each other, however, especially if members of the group have made friends and worked well together. So make sure that an appropriate exchange of email addresses or 'whatsapp' groups is initiated before people leave the course. Some people may surprise you by needing to leave early so it's best not to leave the organising of this to the last day of the course! If your institution has a network for alumni, get the group onto it as soon as you can. Providing lists of reading references and of professional organisations is also essential.

F. If You Are Interested in Virtual Learning, in Personal Learning Networks (PLNs)

The ideas in Parts 1 and 2 of this book work here too. This section simply switches the focus from face to face, and paper and pen, or board and marker, to electronic media. With the development of new electronic media, it has become possible for us teachers to join with colleagues and contacts in our own institutions, locally, and internationally and also to include people in our personal learning networks whom we may never have met face to face; might *never* meet face to face; may only rarely come across in webinar chatrooms, via blogs, vlogs, web conferences, or in MOOCs; or have met only once on, say, a short PD course. It also makes it possible to use a platform, whether Facebook, a wiki, or a web site, to gather together links, podcasts, interviews, texts, reading lists, photos, our own and other people's products—all in one virtual place.

To take full advantage of these new possibilities, we need to understand the hardware, software, and connectivity available and to develop our digital literacy. We need this so that we can avoid being swamped by too much information, or misled by dodgy information, and, instead, exploit the range of facilities available safely, privately, and critically in order to build a learning network of people and materials that we trust. This is a huge development opportunity in itself and one that, if grasped, will pay dividends in our work with our own language students. Depending on our preferences, we can tackle this building, over time, of our own personal, virtual resource room—our own multi-media library complete with virtual librarians—alone, with a colleague or two, via PD sessions, via courses, or by discussing and learning from our students. Excellent ways to start this work are available from another book in this series (see Dudeney, Hockly & Pegrum, 2013).

Part 4

From Implementation to Research

A. Two Perspectives on Studying Teacher Development Over Time

Teacher development is both an external and an internal phenomenon. It involves not just changes in actions that are observable, but also shifts in thinking, in attitude, and in grasping the complexities of the work. This combination of inner and outer worlds makes teacher development difficult to study. There are external aspects that can be seen — what the person does in teaching — and there are internal, private aspects that need to be recounted by the individual. The interrelation of the inner and outer dimensions is dynamic and contextual, which makes it even more complicated to study 'over time.'

1. A Research Perspective to Studying Teacher Development 'Over Time'

As described in Part 1, researchers have tended either to study this development longitudinally (as Tsui did) or at scale (as Lortie, Huberman, and the *Learning4Teaching* Project have done). In the first instance, the phrase 'over time' suggests gathering data on teachers' work over extended periods, as Tsui did in her study where she followed the four teachers for several months (see Freeman, 1996 for an example). These sustained studies are relatively straightforward to design; the focus is usually on a few teachers, and the data-gathering generally involves interviews and observations conducted over time. They can be challenging to carry out, however. Like any continued endeavour, staying with a teacher through weeks, months, or even years of teaching is complex. Inevitably things will change in both the lives and work of the teacher and the researcher, and what might have seemed fairly clear-cut in the planning stages can become messy and disconnected as it unfolds through the school term or year.

Due in part to these complexities of scheduling, longitudinal studies are generally by their nature small-scale. They often result in case studies, as Tsui's did, which present textured examinations of one or a few teachers' work. The power of these studies lies in their authenticity; readers can often plausibly see themselves in the researchers' accounts. These judgments that readers make about a piece of research are what is conventionally referred to as 'validity', in essence readers' judgments about whether the study's findings are meaningful and believable. The meaningfulness of findings usually stems from their realism, so their validity depends on how 'true' the reader thinks the description is. Qualitative researcher Joseph Maxwell argues that, validity in this type of work is defined by the relationship between "the account [the research study] and something outside or external to it—that is, the phenomenon the account is *about*" (1992, p. 283, original italics). Words from the interviews and descriptions from the observations ring true to the reader when they capture the context and the activity of specific classrooms and the teaching that happens in them.

This specificity can also be a source of challenge to these kinds of studies, however. Arguments are sometimes made that the findings are not generalisable across teachers and settings precisely because they are so specific. An alternative to case studies are large-scale research studies that assemble data from many individual teachers to draw wider conclusions about their experience. Part 1 includes three examples of large-scale studies:

- Lortie's study, which used two large data sets of interviews from New England and Dade County, Florida, in the United States.

- Huberman's study combined interviews and observations of groups of teachers from the Swiss Cantons of Geneva and Vaud with different years of teaching experience.

- The *Learning4Teaching* Project organised national-level data sets on ELT professional development in three different countries.

Research designs such as these allow the researchers to look across a wide variety of instances in order to compile meaningful patterns in teacher development over time.

In these types of large-scale studies, validity is based on the representativeness of the sample, in other words the degree to which the teachers who took part in the study are similar to teachers in the context more broadly. The strength of large-scale studies often seems to come from their archetypal quality. The broad patterns in their findings capture things that are true across individuals and situations. In the *Learning4Teaching* Project for example, as explained in Part 1, the analyses describe patterns in professional development events that go beyond the particulars of any specific event. In this approach, teachers described the professional development they did in their own words, and then the researchers combined qualitative and statistical analytic means to identify patterns across the rich variety of these descriptions. These patterns represent, in effect, national archetypes of ELT teachers' views of professional development events in these national contexts.

The two approaches to studying teacher development over time differ in basic, and very useful ways, as represented in Figure 4.1. *Large-scale studies*, on the left, compile individual instances (represented by the dotted circles) to meaningfully 'represent' the broader experiences of the groups studied. *Longitudinal studies*, across the bottom, look at specific

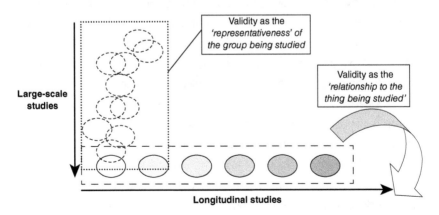

Figure 4.1 Two approaches to validity in studies 'over time'

instances over time (represented by the shaded circles) to capture the complexity of teaching.

Summarising the Research Perspective

Longitudinal studies, by definition, use time as the main variable. By following individuals and capturing their experiences through interviews and observations, these studies document—and thus represent— development 'over time'. Large-scale studies, in contrast, collapse the 'over time' dimension by studying multiple examples at different chronological points. Each view makes a particular argument for the validity of studies done in this way, why they are credible and ought to be believed. In longitudinal research designs, the validity comes in the *relationship* between the study and the phenomenon of teacher development over time. In large-scale studies, validity comes from the degree to which the sample of teachers who are studied and their experiences are *representative of* the broader population. In both types of study however, validity is a judgment made by those who are consuming the research. In other words, no study is 'valid' in-and-of-itself; its validity depends on the readers' judgments, which are based in their experiences and what matters to them.

Researching teacher development usually takes an external perspective, if only because the researcher and the teacher are different people. Lortie's study, for example, captured teachers' views over time through interviews in their own words, although the final account was prepared by the researcher. Huberman and Tsui documented participants' views and experiences through interviews and observations, but *they* then told the stories as researchers. Similarly, the research in the *Learning4Teaching* Project concentrated on how teachers described the professional development they did (as well as what they learned, and how they used it in their classrooms) in their own words. These are studies of teacher development from the outside-in—what is sometimes called an 'etic' perspective. The alternative, of course, is to study teacher development from the inside-out—'the emic' perspective. There are ways that teachers can and do study their own development, which we turn to now.

2. An Inquiry Perspective—Studying Your Own Development as a Teacher 'Over Time'

Of course the alternative to researchers studying teachers is for teachers themselves to study and document their own development. This section describes that process; in writing it, we use 'you' to refer to you, the teacher-reader, and 'we' to refer to us as authors. As a practitioner, you can ask:

> *What are questions that you can (or want to) ask about your life as a teacher over time? How can you study these questions—for yourself and perhaps for others?*

Questions in this vein immediately raise issues of procedure, of how to study your own teaching. The usual response has been to direct teachers to research through procedural vehicles such as action research, classroom research, or teacher-research. A great deal has been written about these approaches (Brumfit and Mitchell, 1989, Freeman, 1998, Burns, 2010.) While they differ in important ways, each of these approaches can be very useful depending on the circumstances and the goals of the endeavour. Table 4.1 summarises the main distinctions.

While these three approaches share some key characteristics, like the immediate focus on classrooms and the teaching and learning in them, action research, classroom research, and teacher-research differ in subtle ways in their goals and how they are structured procedurally. However, they focus mainly on the externals of teaching—what is happening for students and their learning in the classroom—and how to understand and possibly improve it. The approaches are less likely to be concerned specifically with the internal world of teacher's experiences, how that internal world may change longitudinally over time, and how it contributes to and influences student learning.

From Implementation to Research

Table 4.1 Classroom research, Action research, Teacher research

	Classroom research	Action research	Teacher-research
Focuses on	what is happening in the **classroom**, usually related to student learning	how to **understand and improve specific aspects of teaching** and/or to **influence student learning**	using what is done in teaching **to better understand and improve students' learning**
Aims to	document and understand classroom phenomena	improve conditions and outcomes of teaching/ teacher's work for better student learning	generate knowledge about teaching/learning from the teacher's perspective
Participants	students, the teacher, often with the help of an outside researcher	students and teacher	students and teacher
Time Frame	determined by the study (see Nunan and Bailey, 2009)	iterative, with cycles of study driven by the teacher's circumstances (see Burns, 2010)	determined by the teacher within the circumstances of work (see Freeman, 1998)

In Part 4, as authors we take a somewhat different approach, one that connects to the original impetus for the research studies we discussed in Part 1. In these studies, the researchers asked teachers about their experiences of their work. As we said, this approach articulates an 'emic' (or insider's) view of teaching. Similarly, when you do the asking of yourself as a teacher, when you inquire into your own development, you do so from an emic point of view. You are inquiring of yourself about your experiences of teaching and how these have evolved. Time becomes the backdrop; it provides the framework through which you see yourself; you locate changes; you identify key turning points; and you understand how your past experiences are contributing to who you are and what you do as a teacher in the present.

As exemplified by the practical activities in Part 2 and the discussion in Part 3 about ways to integrate them into the full-time work of teaching, these inquiries can be undertaken in several different ways. Below, we have organised the inquiries into three broad areas: *working collectively*, *working with fellow teachers*, or *working on your own*. The social structures that support you differ in each of these areas, but the focus is always defined by you as the teacher.

B. Inquiring Collectively

This approach harnesses the saying that there is 'strength in numbers'. By working as a group of teachers to focus on patterns and themes in your collective experience, the goal is to examine what is *common* among all of your experiences. For instance, you can focus on:

- *A particular point in time or in your careers* (maybe as first-year teachers or approaching retirement);

- *Specific aspects of teaching* (like doing project work, or maybe teaching extensive reading, for example);

- *A particular teaching context or working with a specific group of students* (maybe the final year of secondary school, or a particular group of students on a summer course);

- *A given outcome* (maybe an important milestone, such as a national exam, or a transition, such as moving from middle to secondary school, for example).

In each focus described above (or whatever others you might choose), you are using your collective experience as the vehicle for the inquiry. In this sense, it becomes a process of comparing notes about what everyone is thinking or doing with regard to the focus. In this process, you may begin to surface certain assumptions that may be shared in your thinking and/or common features of actions you take in this situation. You can then step back from this collective experience to examine it, to ask why you collectively think or do these things. In this way, the experience provides the 'text' and the discussion and examination becomes the means of inquiring into it.

Using Ideas and Activities as a Possible Focus

The ideas in Part 1 as well as the activities in Part 2 can provide alternative ways to focus this type of collective inquiring. You can use a theme taken from the research discussed in Part 1 as a lens for examining your collective experience. Taking Lortie's discussion of the tension between autonomy and isolation as a theme, for example, as a group you could compare notes around questions such as, *To what degree does this theme seem accurate in our experience? Do we experience this tension in our work as teachers? If so, how and when? If not, why not?* Alternatively, you can use the questions about past, present, and future in Part 2 in a similar way, to scaffold thinking about patterns in your development over time. These two strategies use ideas taken from Parts 1 or 2 as labels to surface issues that you can consider and discuss collectively. In this way, the themes (in Part 1) along with questions (in Part 2) offer a sort of common vocabulary of ideas that can become a shared platform for discussing collective experience. Reflecting in this way can help you to identify a common topic or theme to research further.

Creating a Common Starting Point—a 'Text From Experience'

Another way to get started on a collective inquiry is to create a common text from your classrooms. These texts can be visual; they can use classroom work, or they might be based on peers observing classes. The following sections elaborate these ideas.

Visuals

At the beginning of your work together, the group can decide to each take three or four **photos** of some aspect of their class. You might choose:

- A common point in the lesson (like the opener or ice-breaker).

- A particular perspective (perhaps photos of the whole class from the front of the room just after the teacher has asked the whole class a question).

- A certain type of interaction (maybe students in pairs doing a task).

- The physical features of the classroom, such as the room layout.

Classroom Work

Secondly, in a similar fashion, the group can agree to use **student work or classroom products** as a starting point for collective inquiry. Each teacher brings a small subset of marked student work (maybe two of the 'best' responses, two in the middle range, and two 'weak' examples) of a particular assignment. (It often works best if the examples are kept anonymous, since the focus is on students and their learning. To do so, the assignments should be tagged in such a way that teachers only know which ones they themselves contributed. They are then shuffled into a collective set.) The group reads the exemplars and discusses similarities, perhaps in how students treated the topic chosen, or the length and complexity of their responses, or what makes a 'good' or a 'weak' example. The group can also turn to the teaching dimension, to discuss the marking scheme and policies, or maybe how the amount of homework done by students affects the results.

Peer Observation

Finally, a slightly more involved but highly productive way to create a shared text of experience is for everyone in the group to ask a peer from outside the group to observe a lesson. The group agrees in advance to have these peer observers use the same observation task—for example, to look at classroom participation—marking the number of times girls or boys are called on in class or the number of times each gender offers or initiates contributions; or wait time— how long the teacher waits after a question before either calling on a student or a student volunteers an answer (and which gender is called on or answers). The observation data can be displayed in a simple chart, and again anonymity is often best.

Working With 'a Common Text'—Analysing, Describing, Interpreting

In each case, once the common text has been made public (posting the photos, reading through the student work, posting the peer observation data), the group examines it for patterns and differences. These discussions often work most effectively if you start with general impressions, allowing everyone a chance to comment, and then get into more specifics. Then in discussing the specifics, it's useful to distinguish between comments based on the information (which we might call 'observations' about the data) and comments that infer meaning (which we could call 'interpretations'). In this basic distinction, the group ought to be able to generally agree on the 'observations', while there may be several different and alternative 'interpretations'.

Below are some questions that can guide these conversations:

*   What stands out for you across the various examples? What pat-terns or commonalities do you see? What differences? Are there any

outliers—aspects that stand out as different or outside the pattern—
that you notice? [Observations]

- How would you interpret this pattern/commonality/difference/out-
lier? Why do you think it is happening? [Interpretations]

- Have you seen this pattern/commonality/difference/outlier in other
classes? . . . at other points in your teaching? [Interpretation]

C. Inquiring With Fellow Teachers

A second way to work with fellow teachers is as peers, supporting
one another to individually inquire into issues and facets of your
development. In contrast to inquiring collectively, where the focus is
on shared experiences, inquiring with peers uses the social aspect to
support your individual thinking. There are several procedures that can
support this kind of socialised inquiry; 'critical friends' is one that is
widely used in schools in the United States (Appleby, 1998; Cushman,
1998). Developed by the Annenberg Institute for School Reform at
Brown University (see www.annenberginstitute.org), the protocols for
groups to work together have become part of a grass-roots professional
development movement called the National School Reform Faculty (see
www.nsrfharmony.org).

The *Critical Friends Process* is generally done with groups of four to
seven teachers so that everyone can participate easily. (See Appendix
for a description.) Like other teacher-inquiry activities, the procedure,
which they call a 'consultancy', is based on defined roles. These
include:

- The *facilitator*, who monitors the group to make sure it follows the
steps of the procedure. This person does not participate directly in
the discussion, but keeps track of time (and adjusts it as needed), and
makes sure that everyone has a chance to be heard.

- The *presenter*, whose teaching is the focus of the 'consultancy'.

- The *discussants*, who are the other members of the group.

From Implementation to Research

After the facilitator reviews the protocol and roles, the presenter introduces an issue from their classroom. The presenter "share(s) an issue, and members of the Critical Friends group offer 'warm' and 'cool' feedback, talking to each other [and] not to the person who presented the issue. The presenter sits outside the group, listening, taking notes, and deciding what has been useful" (Critical Friends Process, p. 2).

This specific format—the presentation, followed by stepping outside the group's discussion—is key in creating a 'consultative' process that focuses on the issue rather than the teacher who is presenting it. The protocol notes, "Unlike most discussions of this nature, the presenter does not participate in the group discussion. [He or she] sits outside the group and does not maintain eye contact during the discussion" (Critical Friends Process, p. 2).

We include this description of the Critical Friends 'consultative' process here (rather than as an activity in Part 2) because it illustrates several points that are central to harnessing the social dynamics of the group to inquire with peers. Teachers often talk about teaching in many social contexts—in the coffee or lunch break, in the teachers' room, sometimes at staff meetings, or perhaps with fellow teachers on the commute to or from work. These opportunities, although they take different forms, tend to share certain features:

- They generally *happen spontaneously*.

- The *interactions* follow the social norms of the activity or event.

- *Roles* can be ambiguous—Who has the floor? What can/should others say? How are they meant to respond?

- The *goal* is not clearly stated—What is supposed to be happening?

- The *outcome* (if any) is usually unclear—What is the take-away? A spontaneous conversation with a colleague can be enormously helpful; more often than not, however, it becomes water over the dam, lost in the flow of work.

Inquiring with peers is a way to harness the energy of these social interactions and spontaneous conversations by using an agreed-upon procedural protocol that defines each of the points above. For example, the Critical Friends 'consultative' process is planned; the protocol describes specific roles that are meant to define how the group interactions unfold; the goal—to focus on the teaching and not the person of the teacher—is underscored by the fact the presenter sits outside the group. Most crucially, the outcome is socialised. The presenting teacher is meant to get something from the 'critical' consideration of their teaching issue; and as 'friends', group members are likely to take away insights from the discussion.

There are other procedures similar in intent and in structure to Critical Friends (see, for example, the description of Teacher Knowledge Inquiry Groups in Rodgers, 2002 and Graves, 2009). These procedures share the goal of drawing on what Lee Shulman called the 'wisdom of practice' of fellow teachers to inquire into an issue or aspect in teaching. In this way, peers become a resource; they do not 'solve' the problem. Any decision to act on their suggestions or to use their ideas remains firmly with the teacher who introduces the issue. This is the essence of inquiring with peers.

Here again there are several activities in Part 2 that could launch or support the process of inquiring with peers—for example, *Critical Incidents* (Activity 9), *Building Case Studies* (Activity 28), *Freirean Problem Posing* (Activity 29), *Teaching Bump* (Activity 30). Similarly, the general steps outlined in the earlier section titled 'Creating a Common Starting Point—'A Text from Experience' can easily be modified to focus on one member of the group. In this case, for example, the 'presenting teacher' would prepare the photo collage, or select and bring the set of student work, or even share the peer observation data. The focus would then be concretely on this person's teaching, which can create both potential openings and possible vulnerabilities. Like the Critical Friends process, it is important to circle back to all members of the group so that while the focus and discussion may centre on one person, the insights and questions are taken up across the group.

D. Inquiring on Your Own

A third alternative is to undertake inquiries into your development working as an individual on your own. This form of individual inquiring can start with different aspects of your work and experience as discussed in the previous sections, and the process is similar to inquiring collectively or with fellow teachers. It starts with questions about something in your work as a teacher. These are generally *why* questions, which launch an inquiry into your own reasoning and thinking, as distinct from *what* or *how* questions, which often anchor action research or teacher-research. In asking yourself *why*, you can set up a process that probes what you assume (and perhaps take for granted) in your experiences. From generating these initial questions, the process, depicted in Figure 4.2, moves to gathering information about them, and then on this basis to challenging your assumptions.

In **generating questions**, you are asking about what matters to you as a teacher. What do you care about? And why does it matter to you now, in this teaching situation, at this point in your career? In Part 2, *From Tactics to Beliefs* (Activity 31), *Yearly Retrospective* (Activity 8), and *How Can I Check My Pedagogical Competence?* (Activity 20) are examples of activities that can help to generate questions from your teaching.

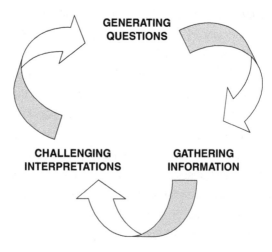

Figure 4.2 Inquiring into teaching

The questions, unlike those that are usually the focus of action research or teacher-research, are about you as a teacher. You are using your experiences to better understand what matters to you in your work with students, colleagues, and the wider professional community.

When you move to the next step, to **gathering information**, you focus on the sources of information that can respond to—and possibly illuminate—these questions. Often the closest and best sources of information are your students and your colleagues. Asking them can engage the issue from various perspectives. For example, you may be feeling you are in a rut, that you are doing the same things in class without much investment or pleasure. You question how your teaching is being experienced by others. You gather information, perhaps through oral or written feedback, or maybe by asking students to draw a picture of the class as they experience it. You then tally that information, looking for themes and patterns in the feedback, or common features in the drawings.

The information you have collected and digested can then lead to **challenging your interpretations**. How could you be misunderstanding what is going on here? What are ways that you might be mistaken? You could ask some fellow teachers, 'I'm wondering whether routine is taking over my teaching. I've gotten some information from my students and this is what I think they're saying. What would you say? What could I not be seeing here? How might I be wrong?'

E. Starting the Process

The beauty of researching your development over time is that you can start this process of inquiring into your experience at any point in your career or at any point in your teaching year. You could *gather some information*, and then *examine how you interpret the situation* from this information, which in turn may *generate questions*. Or you might *start from your interpretation*—what you think is happening—and then look at the *questions it generates* for you, and *information in response* to these questions that might elaborate, confirm, or challenge that interpretation.

From Implementation to Research

Wherever you choose to start and however you choose to proceed—on collective issues, with fellow teachers or on your own—the process of inquiring can open up understanding of how you have developed and are developing as a teacher over time. As the poet, T.S. Eliot, says, in his poem 'Little Gidding', exploration drives this sense of discovery, and at the end of it all we often see what is familiar in new ways, as if for the first time.

Critical Friends: A Process Built on Reflection

Introduction

The Critical Friends process focuses on developing collegial relationships, encouraging reflective practice, and rethinking leadership. This process is based in cooperative adult learning, which is often contrary to patterns established in work environments. It also addresses a situation in which many leaders find themselves—trained to work as independent units; certified as knowing all that is needed to know; feeling like the continuation of professional learning is not essential to the creation of an exciting, rich, learning environment; and that they are simply supervisors in the leadership role.

'Critical' in the context of the group is intended to mean 'important' or 'key' or 'necessary'. Those who have used this process have found that many leaders are clumsy at being 'critical'. They have further discovered that many leaders are trained to talk around and avoid difficult issues, not carefully confront them. The Critical Friends process provides an opportunity both to solicit and provide feedback in a manner that promotes reflective learning.

Background

The Annenberg Institute for School Reform at Brown University first developed the Critical Friends model for collegial dialogue. It is currently in use by an estimated 35,000 teachers, principals, and college professors in over 1,500 schools. In July 2000, the National School Reform Faculty program, which currently houses Critical Friends Groups and coordinates the training for Critical Friends Coaches, relocated to the Harmony School Education Center (HSEC) in Bloomington, Indiana.

Critical Friends: A Process Built on Reflection

As originally developed, the three 'occasions' for reflection using the Critical Friends protocol are: (1) peer observations; (2) tuning a teaching artefact using the Tuning Process; or (3) consulting about an issue using the Consultancy Process. Each activity in the Critical Friends group contains elements of careful description, enforced thoughtful listening, and then questioning feedback—which may well be the basic elements of reflection. The feedback arrived at through the discussions also has been grouped in these ways: 'warm' feedback consists of supportive, appreciative statements about the work presented; 'cool' or more distanced feedback offers different ways to think about the work presented and/or raises questions; and 'hard' feedback challenges and extends the presenter's thinking and/or raises concerns. In general, this process utilises time limits and agreed-upon purpose and norms help reduce interruptions in discussion and the rush-to-comment approach that our busy lives seem to promote.

The basic format for collegial dialogue is the same for each protocol: facilitator overview; presentation of observations, work, or issue; clarification questions; feedback/discussion by participants (discussants); presenter reflection; debriefing of process. The questions and issues that presenters offer typically spring from feelings of concern, from moments in work without closure, and from issues they have not been able to find a solution for through solitary thinking. The focus in our workshop will be on the Consultancy Process.

There are three roles in the Critical Friends process: facilitator, presenter, and discussants. The group can vary in size from four to seven people.

Group Member Roles

Facilitator

Reviews the process at the outset, even if everyone is familiar with it. Sets time limits and keeps time carefully. Participates in discussions but is on the lookout for others who want to get in conversations.

Adjusts time slightly depending on participation. May end one part early or extend another, but is aware of the need to keep time. Reminds discussants of roles, warm and cool feedback, and keeping on topic that the presenter designated. Leads debriefing process and is careful about not 'shorting' this part. Is careful during the debriefing not to slip back into discussion.

Presenter

Prepares an issue for consultancy. Is clear about the specific questions that should be addressed. Unlike most discussions of this nature, the presenter does not participate in the group discussion. Sits outside the group and does not maintain eye contact during the discussion but rather takes notes and gauges what is helpful and what is not. Later, is specific about the feedback that was helpful.

Discussants

Address the issue brought by the presenter and give feedback that is both warm (positive) and cool (critical). The feedback should be given in a supportive tone and discussants should provide practical suggestions.

The 'Consultancy' Process

The consultancy process allows colleagues to share issues confidentially and seek suggestions for positively overcoming or managing them. Consultancy creates opportunities for colleagues to find ways collaboratively around the obstacles and barriers that often limit or stifle effective action.

The process works best in smaller groups (four to seven people) where colleagues can feel comfortable sharing complex issues. Presenters share an issue, and members of the Critical Friends group offer 'warm' and 'cool' feedback, talking to each other not to the person who presented the issue. The presenter sits out of the group, listening, taking

Critical Friends: A Process Built on Reflection

notes, and deciding what has been useful. The actual process (with maximum time allotted) follows.

Step 1: Facilitator Overview (3 minutes)

- Review process
- Set time limits

Step 2: Presenter Overview (5 minutes)

- Share issue
- Provide context
- Frame key question for specific consideration

Step 3: Probing or Clarifying Questions (5 minutes)

- Group members ask more questions to learn about the issue
- Reminder: This is not a time to give advice or get into the discussion

Step 4: Discussant's Group Discussion (12 minutes)

- Group discusses issue (both warm and cool)
- Presenter is silent, taking notes
- Group addresses possible suggestions related to the issue

Step 5: Presenter Response (5 minutes)

- Presenter responds to group feedback

Step 6: Debriefing (5 minutes)

- Facilitator leads discussion, critiquing the process

References and Further Reading

Appleby, J. (1998). *Becoming critical friends: Reflections of an NSRF coach*. Providence, RI: The Annenberg Institute for School Reform at Brown University.
Bambino, D. (March, 2002). Redesigning professional development: Critical friends. *Educational Leadership, 59*(6), 25–27.
Cushman, K. (May, 1998). *How friends can be critical as schools make essential changes*. Oxon Hill, MD: Coalition of Essential Schools.

Note: Other articles and materials were used to create this document; unfortunately, many of the materials used in this compilation did not have identifying information and therefore it was impossible to cite the original source.

Resources

Annenberg Institute for School Reform: www.annenberginstitute.org/

Critical Friends Groups at the National School Reform Faculty, which is a professional development initiative of the Harmony School Education Center in Bloomington, Indiana: www.harmony.pvt.k12.in.us/www/cfg1.html

Preparing an Issue for Consultancy: A Guide for Presenters

Not sure if you have any issues to present? Consider:

Ever wonder if you took the appropriate action?

Challenged by a particular employee and not sure how to proceed?

Looking for fresh ideas or a different approach to a challenging dilemma?

Not sure how to follow up with an issue that needs to be addressed?

Recently been 'stumped' by a situation?

Critical Friends: A Process Built on Reflection

These are precisely the issues that you could bring to the 'Presenters' table through the Critical Friends Consultancy process.

Framing the Issue

It is important to provide the discussants with enough information to discuss effectively and create solutions for the issue you are presenting. As you prepare your issue, consider including the following:

- Context in which the issue presents itself—does this situation come up in department meetings, or is this related to a philosophical disagreement in a particular discipline?

- Important components surrounding the case—past history between the actors, or personnel structures that affect your ability to act.

- If there is a meta issue looming behind the issue you present, it would be useful to share that with the discussants.

- Your actions and/or reactions about the issue.

- What you would like the group to discuss or the outcome you seek from the discussants—alternate suggestions, reinforcement for your actions, identify potential obstacles for you, and so on.

Preparing to Present

Consider bringing notes to the meeting at which you present. Remember that you only have 5 minutes to present your issue. Discussants do have 5 minutes to ask you clarifying questions, but that is really time for them to get a better idea of the scenario. It is very important to let the group know what you want to get as a result from their discussion.

Following Your Presentation

Listen carefully; take notes. Often the discussants will try to bring you back into the group, but it is more useful if you are able to distance yourself from the discussants so that you can capture all the information discussed. Hold yourself back from making judgments during the discussion as this might affect your ability to hear all the ideas and feedback.

For the Presenter Response

This time portion is your opportunity to respond to the group discussion. This is not the time to continue the discussion with you involved. This is an opportunity for you to summarise your impressions of the discussion. Consider all the information gathered and identify which ideas might be useful and which ones you are unlikely to pursue.

References

Allwright, D. (1996). Social and pedagogic pressures in the language classroom: The role of socialisation. In H. Coleman (Ed.), *Society and the language classroom* (pp. 209–228). Cambridge: Cambridge University Press.

Appleby, J. (1998). *Becoming critical friends: Reflections of a national school reform faculty coach*. Providence, RI: The Annenberg Institute for School Reform at Brown University.

Archer, C. (1986). Culture bump and beyond. In J. M. Valdes (Ed.), *Culture bound: Bridging the cultural gap in language teaching* (pp. 170–178). Cambridge: Cambridge University Press.

Ball, S., & Goodson, L. (1985). *Teachers' lives and careers*. London: Falmer Press.

Bennett, T. (2013). *Teacher proof: Why research in education doesn't always mean what it claims, and what we can do about it*. Abingdon, Oxon: Routledge.

Bereiter, C., & Scardamalia, M. (1993). *Surpassing ourselves: An inquiry into the nature and implications of expertise*. Chicago, IL: Open Court.

Berlak, A., & Berlak, E. (1981). *The dilemmas of schooling*. London: Methuen.

Berliner, D. C. (1992). The nature of expertise in teaching. In F. Oser, A. Dick & J. Patry (Eds.), *Effective and responsible teaching: The new synthesis* (pp. 227–248). San Francisco, CA: Jossey-Bass.

Berliner, D. C. (1994). The wonder of exemplary performances. In J. N. Margieri & C. C. Block (Eds.), *Creating powerful thinking in teachers and students' diverse perspectives* (pp. 161–186). Fort Worth, TX: Harcourt Brace College.

Berliner, D. C. (1995). The development of pedagogical expertise. In P. K. Siu & P. T. K. Tam (Eds.), *Quality in education: Insights from different perspectives* (pp. 1–14). Hong Kong: Hong Kong Educational Research Association.

Brumfit, C., & Mitchell, R. (Eds.). (1989). *Research in the language classroom*. British Council: ELT Documents #133.

Burns, A. (2010). *Doing action research in English language teaching*. New York: Routledge.

Buzan, T. (2009). *The mind map book: Unlock your creativity, boost your memory, change your life*. London: BBC Active.

Carroll, L. (1865). *Alice's adventures in wonderland*. New York: D. Appleton and Company.

Church, M. (1997). The parable of the good language learner. *The Teacher Trainer*, *11*(3), 9.

Clandinin, D. (1986). *Classroom practice: Teacher images in action*. London: Falmer Press.

Clark, C. (2001). *Talking Shop: Authentic conversation and teacher learning*. New York: Teachers College Press.

Coburn, C. E. (2005). Shaping teacher sense-making: School leaders and the enactment of reading policy. *Educational Policy*, *19*(3), 476–509.

Coburn, C. E., & Stein, M. K. (2006). Communities of practice theory and the role of teacher professional community in policy implementation. In M. Honig (Ed.), *New directions in education policy implementation: Confronting complexity*. (pp. 25–49). New York, SUNY Press.

Cohen, D. K. (2011). *Teaching and its predicaments*. Cambridge, MA: Harvard University Press.

Cohen, J., McCabe, L., Michelli, N. M., & Pickeral, T. (2009). School climate: Research, policy, practice, and teacher education. *Teachers College Record*, *111*(1), 180–213.

Cosh, J. (1998). Peer observation in higher education—a reflective approach. *Innovations in Education & Training International*, *35*(2), 171–176.

Critical Friends' protocol. https://depts.washington.edu/ccph/pdf_files /Critical-Friends.pdf

Cushman, K. (1998). *How friends can be critical as schools make essential changes*. Oxon Hill, MD: Coalition of Essential Schools.

De Bono, E. (1985). *Six thinking hats*. Boston: Little Brown.

Desimone, L. (2009). Improving impact studies of teachers' professional development: toward better conceptualizations and measures. *Educational Researcher*, *38*(3), 181–199.

Dudeney, G., Hockly, N., & Pegrum, M. (2013). *Digital literacies*. Harlow, UK: Pearson.

Dunkin, M., & Biddle, B. (1974). *The study of teaching*. New York: Holt, Rinehart and Winston.

Elbaz, F. (1983). *Teacher thinking: A study of practical knowledge*. New York: Nichols.

Erikson, E. H. (1950). *Childhood and society*. New York: Norton.

Fanselow, J. (1987). *Breaking rules: Generating and exploring alternatives in language teaching*. New York: Pearson. Also available (2012). CreateSpace Independent Publishing Platform.

Freeman, D. (1996). Renaming experience/reconstructing practice: Developing new understandings of teaching. In D. Freeman & J. C. Richards (Eds.), *Teacher learning in language teaching* (pp. 221–241). New York: Cambridge University Press.

Freeman, D. (1998). *Doing teacher-research: from inquiry to understanding*. Boston: Heinle Cengage

Freeman, D. (2016). *Educating second language teachers: The same things done differently*. Oxford: Oxford University Press.

Freeman, D., & Graves, K. (2013). Studying teacher professional development "at scale": What we can learn about connections between policy, implementation, and experience. *The Teacher Trainer*, *27*(3), 2–6.

Freeman, D., Reynolds, D., Toledo, W., & Al-Tineh, A. (2017). Who provides professional development? A study of ELT professional development in Qatar. *Iranian Journal of Language Teaching Research*, *4*(3), 5–19.

Garcia-Stone, A. (2017). Professional development late in a teaching career. Part Two. *The Teacher Trainer*, *31*(1), 17–19.

References

Graves, K. (2000). *Designing language courses: A guide for teachers*. Boston: Heinle Cengage.

Graves, K. (2009). Collaborating for autonomy in teaching and learning. In T. Yoshida, H. Imai, Y. Nakata, A. Tajino, O. Takeuchi & K. Tamai (Eds.), *Researching language teaching and learning: An integration of practice and theory* (pp. 159–179). Oxford: Peter Lang.

Griffin, M. L. (2003). Using critical incidents to promote and assess reflective thinking in preservice teachers. *Reflective Practice, 4*(2), 207–220.

Huberman, M. (1989). The professional life cycles of teachers. *Teachers College Record, 91*(1), 31–57.

Huberman, M. (1991). Teacher development and instructional mastery. In A. Hargreaves & M. Fullan (Eds.), *Understanding teacher development* (pp. 171–195). London: Cassells.

Huberman, M., Grounauer, M., & Marti, J. (1993). *The lives of teachers*. London: Cassell.

Isoré, M. (2009). *Teacher evaluation: Current practices in OECD countries and a literature review*. OECD Education Working Papers, No. 23. OECD Publishing.

Jackson, P. (1968). *Life in Classrooms*. New York: Teachers College Press.

Jarvis, J. (1991). Perspectives on the in-service training needs of NNS teachers of English to young learners. *The Teacher Trainer, 5*(1), 4–9.

Lampert. M. (1985). How do teachers manage to teach? *Perspectives of Problems of Practice, Harvard Educational Review, 55*(20), 178–194.

Larsen-Freeman, D., & Anderson, M. (2011). *Techniques and principles in language teaching*. New York: Oxford University Press.

Larsen-Freeman, D., & Freeman, D. (2008). Language moves: The place of "foreign" languages in classroom teaching and learning. *Review of Research in Education, 32*, 147–186.

Lave, J., & Wenger, E. (1991). *Situated learning: Legitimate peripheral participation*. Cambridge: Cambridge University Press.

Lemov, D. (2015). *Teach like a champion 2.0*. San Francisco, CA: Jossey-Bass.

Lewin Jones, J. (2017). Signs of motivation: Using a visual stimulus for emotion-focused discussion in teacher training. *The Teacher Trainer, 31*(1), 24–25.

Lortie, D. (1975). *Schoolteacher: A sociological study*. Chicago: University of Chicago Press.

Mansfield, C., Beltman, S., Broadley, T., & Weatherby, N. (2016). Building resilience in teacher education: An evidenced informed framework. *Teaching and Teacher Education, 54*, 77–87.

March, J. and H. Simon. (1958). *Organizations*. New York: Wiley.

Maxwell, J. (1992). Understanding and validity in qualitative research. *Harvard Educational Review, 62*(3), 279–301.

Nunan, D., & K. Bailey (2009). *Exploring second language classroom research: A comprehensive guide*. Boston: Heinle Cengage.

Peyton, J., & Reed, L. (1990). *Dialogue journal writing with nonnative English speakers: A handbook for teachers*. Alexandria, VA: TESOL.

Peyton, J., & Staton, J. (Eds.). (1991). *Writing our lives: Reflections on dialogue journal writing with adults learning English*. Englewood Cliffs, NJ: Regents Prentice Hall and Center for Applied Linguistics.

Peyton, J., & Staton, J. (1993). *Dialogue journals in the multilingual classroom: Building language fluency and writing skills through written interaction.* Norwood, NJ: Ablex.

Rodgers, C. (2002). Seeing student learning and the role of reflection. *Harvard Educational Review, 72*(1), 230–253.

Shulman, L. (1986). Those who understand knowledge growth in teaching. *Educational Researcher, 15*(2), 4–14.

Sikes, P., Measor, L., & Woods, P. (1985). *Teacher careers: Crises and continuities.* London: Falmer Press.

Snoj, J. (February 7, 2017). *Population of Qatar by nationality—2017 report.* http://priyadsouza.com/population-of-qatar-by-nationality-in-2017/ Retrieved February 28, 2017

Spillane, J. P. (1996). School districts matter: Local educational authorities and state instructional policy. *Educational Policy, 10*(1), 63–87.

Stevick, E. (1976). *Memory, meaning and method: A view of language teaching.* Boston: Heinle Cengage.

Stevick, E. (1980). *Teaching languages: A way and ways.* Boston: Heinle Cengage.

Stevick, E. (1990). *Humanism in language teaching: A critical perspective.* Oxford: Oxford University Press.

Tripp, D. (2012). *Critical incidents in teaching: Developing professional judgment.* London: Routledge.

Tsui, A. B. M. (2003). *Understanding expertise in teaching: Case studies of ESL teachers.* Cambridge: Cambridge University Press.

Ur, P. (2016). Why do language teachers need the research? *The Teacher Trainer, 30*(1), 3–5.

Wallerstein, N. (1982). *Language and culture in conflict: Problem-posing in the ESL classroom.* Reading, MA: Addison-Wesley.

Wang, Q. (2007). The national curriculum changes and their effects on English language teaching in the People's Republic of China. In J. Cummins & C. Davison (Eds.), *International handbook of English language teaching* (pp. 87–105). New York: Springer.

Webster-Wright, A. (2009). Reframing professional development through understanding authentic professional learning. *Review of Educational Research, 79*(2), 702–739.

Weintraub, E. (1989). Interview. *The Teacher Trainer, 3*(1), 7–8.

White, E. B. (1952). *Charlotte's web.* New York: Harper Brothers.

Woodward, T. (1991). *Models and metaphors in the foreign language classroom.* Cambridge: Cambridge University Press.

Woodward, T. (1997). Working with teachers interested in different methods. *The Teacher Trainer, 11*(3), 7–9.

Woodward, T. (2001). *Planning lessons and courses.* Cambridge: Cambridge University Press.

Woodward, T. (2004). *Ways of working with teachers.* Elmstone, UK: TW Publications.

Woodward, T. (2006). *Headstrong: A book of thinking frameworks for mental exercise.* Elmstone, UK: TW Publications.

References

Woodward, T. (2011). *Thinking in the EFL class*. Rum, Austria: Helbling Languages.
Woodward, T. (2015). Professional development late in a teaching career. *The Teacher Trainer*, 29(3), 2–3.
Woodward, T., & Lindstromberg, S. (2014). *Something to say*. Rum, Austria: Helbling Languages.

Index

activism 19, 21, 52, 186–187
Allwright, D. 13
Annenberg Institute for School Reform
205, 211. *See also* Critical Friends
Applied Linguistics 157
apprenticeship of observation 4,
9–12, 27, 46–47, 60, 65, 76, 81,
112–113, 184. *See also* Lortie, D.
assessment 12, 43, 135, 160; unclear
criteria for 15–16

Bailey, K. 200
Beloit College Mindset List 112
Bereiter, C. 24, 34
blogs and vlogs 133, 135, 158, 162,
173, 193–194
breaking rules 4, 64, 163–165, 173,
183
British Council, Teaching for Success
174
Burns, A. 199–200
Buzan, T. 100–176

catalytic thinking 102
causal view of professional
development 36–38, 57,
65. *see also* Desimone, L.;
Learning4Teaching Project
Chile, ELT professional development in
36, 40, 58n5, 85–86, 106; 'English
Opens Doors' policy, 38–39, 41, 43;
focus on language competence and
methodology 41, 43; policy-oriented
environment 38–39, 41, 43, 137;
See also Learning4Teaching Project

Church, M. 76
classroom teaching: autonomy vs.
isolation 48, 60, 142, 175, 202;
balancing control and engagement
12, 46; balancing discipline and
student enjoyment 31–32; balancing
social and pedagogical demands
13–14, 49, 54; collaboration
5, 28–29, 35, 134, 146, 189;
discovery and experimentation in
19–23, 26–28, 32–33, 45, 52, 56,
64, 82, 84, 104, 150, 156, 162,
164, 172–173, 184, 187; errors of
avoidance 92–93; group work 5,
14–15, 28, 32, 55, 75, 105–110,
165, 183; maintaining control, work,
and student engagement xv, 10, 12,
29–30, 53, 103; positional authority
of teachers 12, 32; process writing
32–34; relational conditions of 9,
12–14, 19, 21, 46–47, 49, 52, 60,
111, 113, 121; seeking challenges
34–35, 56, 64; and status gains
17; and teachers' knowledge 3,
11, 15–16, 23–24, 26, 28–38,
45, 48, 53–54, 56, 58n2, 63, 84,
91, 95–98, 104, 108,137, 141,
146, 156, 173, 200, 207. *See also*
endemic uncertainty; methodology,
teaching; students, volunteerism;
satisficing
collegiality: inhibiting factors 66,
175; opportunities for, 48, 56; in
professional development 50–51,
61, 66, 211–212. *See also* Critical

223

Index

Friends; dialogue and teacher development
Community Language Learning 74, 83
Counselling Learning 74
craft pride 9, 15–16
Creating a Common Starting Point—A 'Text From Experience' 203–204
Critical differences between novice and expert teachers xiii, 22, 24–26, 28–29, 142
Critical Friends 119, 157, 205–208, 211–217; consultancy 212–213, 215–217; group roles 212–214; peer observations 212; tuning process 212. See also collegiality; professional exchange; Teacher Knowledge Inquiry Groups
critical incidents 31, 53, 55–56, 63, 66, 80–81, 159, 162, 172, 191
culture bump 122
Curran, C. 84. See also Counselling Learning (CL); Community Language Learning (CLL)
curriculum design 5, 12, 14, 30, 32–33, 38, 120, 137, 154–155, 185
curriculum reform 5, 21, 23, 52, 57, 205, 211, 214

de Bono, E. 101–102
Desimone, L. 37–38, 137 See also causal view of professional development.
dialogue and teacher development 50, 61, 119, 175, 211–212. See also collegiality; professional exchange
dialogue journals 51, 63, 73, 89, 92, 110, 113–116, 173, 189–190
dichotomizing teaching knowledge 27, 29, 49, 63, 95–96
discourse communities 35, 48, 141, 186
distributed knowledge/expertise 34–35, 56, 66, 108, 146

egg-crate profession 9, 16, 46–48, 57n4, 60, 66, 175 See also Lortie, D.
Elliot, D. 174
emic (insider's) view of teaching 2–3, 35, 44, 198, 201
endemic uncertainty 13–14
empathy with other teachers 10, 50, 52, 62
English language teaching: for Academic Purposes (EAP) 129; as a Foreign Language (EFL) 25, 54; as lingua franca 39; as a Second Language (ESL) 24, 121, 134; for Special Purposes (ESP) 129
English Language Teaching (ELT) 1, 36; best practices for 96; conferences 130; methods and techniques 41, 43; national environments for 38–39, 41, 43, 197; native vs. non-native speakers and teaching 11, 48, 118; periodicals 174; professional development research 36, 41, 137, 196–197; in the public-sector 6, 35–37, 39–40, 137. See also Learning4Teaching Project; professional development in ELT
etic (outsider's) view of teaching 20, 198
experimentation 20, 23, 27, 33, 45, 52, 82, 173. See also pedagogical tinkering
expertise 3, 5, 48; acquiring 24, 35, 70; definition of 23–25, 35, 48; distinct from experience or seniority 24, 48; distributed 32, 34–35, 56, 66, 108; documentation of 48; experimentation vital to 33, 55–56, 156; integration of knowledge 54, 156; making formal knowledge practical 33; multiple 34, 56, 146; sharing 56, 66, 146; US National Board for Professional Teaching Standards 48

224

expert teachers 23, 25–29, 31–34,
48, 53–54, 80, 82, 105, 182;
becoming expert 24–25, 56;
identifying constraints 125, 127;
integrating teaching knowledge
28–30, 95–96; observing 92, 161;
relationship to teaching contexts
28–31, 54, 142; pedagogical
content knowledge 30, 53–54;
seeking challenges 34; theorising/
practicalising 28–9, 31–33, 45

Fanselow, J. 4, 148, 165. See also
breaking rules
four skills (speaking, reading, writing,
listening) 41, 43
Freeman, D. 6, 35, 44, 58n1,
195, 199–200. See also
Learning4Teaching Project
Freire, P. 119; Freirean problem-
posing 64, 89, 119, 172,
191, 207

gender, power balance in classroom
47, 112, 143, 204; and data
grouping 18
Graves, K. 6, 35. See also
Learning4Teaching Project

Harmony School Education Center
211, 215
Huberman, M. 2–5, 11, 17, 19–25,
27, 33–34, 44–45, 47–53, 55,
57, 59, 61–62, 65–66, 68, 70,
79, 82, 90, 94, 98, 102–104, 111,
123, 147, 150, 153, 158, 163,
173, 181–184, 186–187; activities
based on 59, 61, 68, 70–71, 79,
82, 90–91, 94, 98, 100, 102–104,
111, 123, 147, 150, 153, 158, 163;
Lives of Teachers, The 17–23, 50;
research methods of 6, 17–19,
195–196, 198. See also collegiality;
self-reflection

Huberman, career stages
19–20; Conservatism
19, 21; Disengagement/
Disenchantment 19, 21–22; Easy
or Painful Beginnings 19, 27, 84;
Experimentation/Activism 19–22,
27, 33, 45, 52, 82; Reassessment
20, 22; Relational Distance 19, 21,
52, 111; Self-Doubt 19, 21–22,
26–27; Serenity 19, 21, 166;
Stabilisation 19–20, 22, 27, 51,
158, 163; Survival/Discovery 19–20,
27, 51, 183

Inglés Abre Puertas. See Chile,
'English Opens Doors' policy; ELT
professional development in
in-service courses 4, 24, 44–45, 129
See also Learning4Teaching Project.
inquiring collectively 201–202; on your
own 208–210; into teaching 208,
with other teachers 205–207
inside-out vs. outside-in teaching
profession 9, 16–19, 55
integrating teaching knowledge
28–29, 98

Jackson, P. 7
Jarvis, J. 4

knowledge base and context 29–31,
53–54, 63, 95, 125–128, 142, 156

large-scale research, validity in 197
Learning4Teaching Project 5–6,
42–45, 47, 56–57, 59, 108,
136–137, 195–198; activities based
on 85–86, 106–108, 136–139,
199–204
Learning4Teaching research 35–36,
39–46, 59, 136, 195–199; activities
based on 85–86, 106–108,
137–138, 199–204; inventories of
professional development 36–7;

national surveys of teachers'
experiences, 36–37, 40, 42;
teaching logs 36–7, 40, 106, 108,
137; what teachers learn must be
observable 44
learning outcomes. See outcome-
based education
Lemov, D. 91–92
Lewin Jones, J. 152
literacy, and classroom tasks 30;
digital 194; native languages 119
longitudinal research, validity in 197
long-term career satisfaction 22–23, 52
Lortie, D. 3–4, 6–17, 24–25, 27, 35,
45–51, 56–57, 59–60, 65–66,
76–79, 81, 94–95, 112–113,
121, 128, 133, 141–143, 175,
202, 211–212; activities based on
59–60, 76–77, 81, 94, 112–113,
121, 125, 128, 133, 141–142, 154,
165–166, 175; research methods
of 3, 6–9, 46, 154, 195–196,
198; Schoolteacher 4, 6–8, 15,
46; sociological perspective of 4,
6–8, 13, 45, 47–49, 81. See also
egg-crate profession; endemic
uncertainty; satisficing

making sense: of teaching experience
24, 33, 44, 53, 60, 88, 94–95,
139, 179; of learning opportunities
35–39, 41–42, 44–45, 56–57,
65–66, 86, 136–137
Maxwell, J. 196. See also research
validity
mentoring 104–105, 129, 162,
166–167, 171, 182, 188; reverse
mentoring 184
methodology, teaching 41, 43;
changes in 64, 67, 75–76, 172;
Audio Lingual/Visual Method 74;
Communicative Language Learning
74–75; Community Language
Learning 74–75, 83–85; Direct

Method 74; Dogme 74; Grammar
Translation 74–85; Psychodramatic
Language Learning 74; Silent Way
74; situated learning 25, 30, 54;
Task Based Learning 74. See also
research methodologies
mind mapping 98–100, 155, 193
MOOCs 194

National School Reform Faculty 205

'one-step profession' 9, 16, 46–47,
141, 165–166 See also Lortie, D.
organisation theory 14, 16, 34,
49, 146
outcome-based education theory,
6–7, 12–15, 28

pedagogical competence 66, 68, 78,
102; areas of 103–104; challenges
at the edge of 51, 72, 80, 98, 140;
checking 78, 104, 115, 118–119,
173, 208; developing 40–41, 51,
72, 180–181; and expertise 50–15
pedagogical mastery 66, 78. See also
expertise
pedagogical tinkering 20–23, 27, 52.
See also experimentation
peer observation 92, 143, 162, 181,
183, 186, 192, 204, 207, 212
Personal Learning Environment (PLE)
114, 125
Personal Learning Networks (PLNs)
194
positional authority of teachers 10,
12, 32
practicalising theoretical knowledge
26, 28, 45, 53–56, 63, 64,
104–106
problematising 27, 32–34, 56, 72, 74,
110, 117–121, 130–131. See also
Freire, P.
Professional Certificate in Education
(PCEd) 28, 55

professional development in ELT
36–38, 39, 56–57, 66, 108; across
institutions 186–188; causal view
36–38, 57, 65; conferences 48,
70, 79, 130, 146, 159–160, 181,
185–186, 194; courses 2, 4, 28,
32–33, 35, 43, 86–87, 100, 108,
159–160, 169, 174, 181, 183,
185–186, 188–194; focus on
language competence 41; focus on
methodology 41; and job enrichment
23, 161, 176; keeping a journal
158, 162, 179, 192; national policy
as vernacular language 41; path
model 37–38; as a personal process
56–57, 66 108; and professional
associations 160, 193; sense-making
8, 37–38, 42, 44–45, 56–57, 65–66,
86, 94–95, 137; study groups 48;
teacher websites 159, 180, 193;
talking shop 60, 62, 77–79, 167;
webinars 159–160, 194; workshops
4, 86, 108, 160, 212. See also
Learning4Teaching research
professional development, continuing
(CPD) 48, 158–162, 169, 172, 174,
179–187
professional development, individual
169–175; creativity 172;
experimentation 173; learning from
students 173; mapping career
171–172; reading professional
literature 171, 174; self-reflection
172; teacher training courses 174;
to-do lists 172
professional development, small groups
175–186; discussing shared classes
176–178; doing activities together
176; observing and discussing
teaching 178–179; preparing
presentation together 179; readings
176; resisting isolation 175
professional exchange 48, 88;
improving 193–194

professional learning, modes of 86,
136–139
professional life cycle 5, 17, 19–23,
27, 45, 50–52, 62, 65–66, 70–71,
90, 94, 98, 147, 158, 163, 181,
190. See also Huberman career
stages
public perceptions of teaching 128,
133, 141

Qatar, ELT professional development
in 36, 39–41, 58n5, 85, 106; as a
lingua-franca environment 39 See
also Learning4Teaching Project

relational work of teaching 9, 12–13,
47, 49, 60, 113, 121 See also
Lortie, D.
researching teacher development
over time 195–210; classroom/
action/teacher research 200–201;
establishing validity 196–198;
external vs. internal phenomena
195; group projects 201–205;
individual research 208–210; large-
scale studies 196–198; longitudinal
studies 196–198; peer support and
inquiry 205; self-study 199–201.
See also Critical Friends
research methodologies 2, 6–8;
emic (insiders') perspective 2–3,
35, 44, 198, 201; large-scale
phenomenographic 36; process-
product research 6–7, 15, 44;
qualitative data gathering 7–10, 18,
40, 196–197. See also Huberman,
M.; Learning4Teaching Project;
Lortie, D.; Tsui, A. B. M.
research validity 15, 196–198
resilence 183

satisficing 14–16, 46, 49, 94. See also
Lortie, D.
Scardamalia, M. 24, 34

self-reflection 11, 22, 27, 34, 47,
  49–51, 55, 60–61, 66, 71, 80–81,
  107, 125, 142–143, 156, 172, 182,
  184, 186, 191–192, 202, 211–212.
  See also Critical Friends; satisficing
sense-making 8, 37–38, 42, 44–45,
  56–57, 65–66, 86, 94–95, 137
Shulman, L. 30, 207
Sikes, P. et al. 17
situated teaching and learning 24,
  30, 54
Spanish language 58n6, 97–98
Stevick, E. 13
students 21, 30, 38, 60, 94–95, 127,
  129–132, 152, 170, 200; ability,
  teachers' judgment of 11, 112;
  arousing and sustaining student
  interest 12, 14–15, 28–30, 32, 49,
  103; contact with teachers 10–11;
  discipline and control of 31–32,
  80, 130–133, 164; participation
  in teachers' work 11, 49, 95–96,
  119–121, 139, 200; productive
  learning experiences 34; relational
  conditions of 12–13, 22, 103,
  111–113, 121–125; socialisation
  of 10, 54; teachers learning from
  89, 173, 194, 209; and teaching
  methods 75, 83–84, 87, 90, 92–93,
  95–98, 107, 109–110, 114–116,
  145–146, 203; volunteerism
  13–14. *See also* apprenticeship of;
  classroom teaching
Suggestopedia 74
symbolic interaction theory 10

Teacher Development Special Interest
  Groups 193
Teacher Knowledge Inquiry Groups
  207
teachers' experience: autonomy vs.
  isolation 48, 60, 77–79, 142–143,
  175, 202; making sense of 24, 33,

44, 53, 60, 88, 94–95, 139, 179;
  as students 6, 9–10, 46–47, 60,
  76–79, 81; surveys of teachers'
  experiences 36–37, 40, 42
teacher learning 8–9, 16–19, 43,
  55; approaches to personal
  history 65–66; effects of national
  policy 39, 41; personal practical
  knowledge 28, 31–33, 55, 173;
  practicalising theory 28, 32, 45,
  55; problematising 32, 56, 117,
  119, 130; reframing practice
  55–56; seeking challenges 34–35,
  56, 64; uptake from professional
  development 37, 42, 137. *See
  also* apprenticeship of observation;
  collegiality; experimentation; four
  skills
teachers' perception of their learning
  6, 42–45, 47; national surveys of
  teachers' experiences, 36–37, 40,
  42. *See also Learning4Teaching*
  research
teacher trainers/educators 2, 4, 129,
  143, 167, 169, 174; assessing
  need, 188–189; follow-up 193–194;
  short professional development
  courses 188–194; tangible
  outcomes 192–193
teaching as labour 13–14, 45, 49
teaching logs 36–37, 40, 106,
  108, 137
theorising practical knowledge 26, 28,
  32–34, 55
trajectorists 3–6, 17–18, 50–52, 65,
  62, 65, 71. *See also* Huberman, M.;
  Lortie, D.; Tsui, A. B. M.
Tsui, A. B. M. 3, 5–6, 23–35, 45,
  48, 53–57, 59, 62–64, 66, 95,
  104–106, 108, 117–121, 130–131,
  146; activities based on 34–35,
  62–64, 72, 74, 80, 82, 85, 95–96,
  104–105, 108, 117, 119, 125–128,

130, 142, 144, 146, 152, 156; research methods of 24–26, 195–196, 198; *Understanding Expertise in Teaching* 23. *See also* critical incidents; expertise; expert teachers; practicalising; problematizing; teaching logs
Turkey, ELT professional development in 36, 39–41, 58n5, 85, 87, 106; focus on teaching methods 41–42; socially marketed oriented ELT 39; transforming input into use 43. *See also* Learning4Teaching Project

Ur, P. 157
US National Board for Professional Teaching Standards 48

validity, as judgement 196; as relationship *vs.* as representation 197; in large-scale research, longitudinal research 197. *See also* Maxwell, J.

Woodward, T. 160–162, 168
Working With 'a Common Text' — Analysing, Describing, Interpreting 204–205